Children's Library Services Handbook

Children's Library Services Handbook

by Jane Gardner Connor

ORYX PRESS
1990

The rare Arabian Oryx is believed to have inspired the myth of the unicorn. This desert antelope became virtually extinct in the early 1960s. At that time several groups of international conservationists arranged to have 9 animals sent to the Phoenix Zoo to be the nucleus of a captive breeding herd. Today the Oryx population is nearly 800, and over 400 have been returned to reserves in the Middle East.

Copyright © 1990 by
The Oryx Press
2214 North Central at Encanto
Phoenix, Arizona 85004-1483

Published simultaneously in Canada

Printed and Bound in the United States of America

♾ The paper used in this publication meets the minimum requirements of American National Standard for Information Science—Permanence of Paper for Printed Library Materials, ANSI Z39.48, 1984.

Library of Congress Cataloging-in-Publication Data

Connor, Jane Gardner.
    Children's library services handbook / by Jane Gardner Connor.
        p.   cm.
    Bibliography: p.
    Includes index.
    ISBN 0-89774-489-6
    1. Libraries, Children's—Administration. 2. Children—Books and reading. I. Title.
    Z718.1.C66   1990
    027.62'5—dc20   89-8568
                                                                       CIP

For
Mae Benne
and for
Robert Daniel
and
Gillian Elizabeth
who are part of the future

Contents

Foreword

Those of us who are involved in library services to children are aware of the goals and objectives of this challenging profession. This book tells us how to achieve them. It combines the ideals and philosophy of librarianship with a pragmatic approach, resulting in a realistic how-to manual that's stimulating, inspiring, and invaluable. Jane Gardner Connor communicates a great enthusiasm for the profession, with all its privileges and responsibilities. At the same time, she describes the essential, intrinsic demands of the job and the best ways to meet these demands. Throughout the text there is clear evidence of the commitment required of those who want to enter this field. But commitment alone isn't enough; in these pages we learn of the professional requirements, the skills, talents, and qualifications necessary to ensure good performance as a children's librarian.

Taking into consideration the variety of libraries and variety of people entering the field of librarianship, Ms. Connor covers a wide range of subjects which will be of value to both public and school librarians. Among the topics covered are planning, developing, and maintaining a collection of both print and nonprint materials; management and administration; implementing creative programs utilizing a variety of activities and media, publicity and public relations; and a common-sense approach to the problem of censorship. The excellent, carefully selected bibliographies expand on the basic principles expressed in the text.

Highly readable and well-organized, the book can be utilized as a refresher course for practitioners, a guide for trainees, and as a textbook for library science courses. And as a general manual for children's library services, it deserves a place in every library's children's room.

This book could be subtitled: "Everything you wanted to know about children's librarianship but didn't know where to find it." Well, you can find it here. In one volume, we have all the fundamentals of library service to children. I, for one, am very grateful. No longer will I have to tear around the library seeking articles and journals to form a basic reading list for my students. This much-needed book will serve them well.

Marilyn Kaye
Associate Professor
Division of Library and Information Science
St. John's University, New York

Preface

This book is based on a handbook I wrote in my position as Field Service Librarian for Children's Services at the South Carolina State Library. The original *Children's Services Handbook* was published in 1985 by the South Carolina State Library and was partially funded by Library and Construction Act funds.

The original handbook developed from a need for a basic guide to children's services which could serve as a basis for orientation and training of new children's librarians and other allied personnel. After it was issued, requests for the handbook from around the country indicated a need existed for such a publication.

Children's Library Services Handbook is an expanded and revised version of the original handbook. Its purpose, however, is still to provide an introduction to services for children. Information on the school library media center has been added, with the terms "school library" and "school library media center" used interchangeably. Although this book emphasizes public libraries, school library media centers are also covered because much of the material presented here will be useful to both.

The purpose of this handbook is to put in one place the basics of library service to children. Other excellent books may give a fuller and more complete picture of specific information covered in a particular chapter, and many of these are listed in the bibliographies at the end of each chapter. The emphasis throughout this book is on the practical rather than the theoretical, not only the "whys" of programming, for example, but also the "hows."

Ideally, all librarians working with children would have as a foundation the basic knowledge contained in this book. However, statistics show that this is not true. While over 80 percent of public libraries serve populations of 25,000 or less, many do not have trained children's librarians. Branches often have one person to provide all services. Even urban libraries have fewer trained children's librarians than they once did. Enoch Pratt Public Library in Baltimore now has no more than four or five trained children's librarians for the entire system. Chicago has approximately 40 for 85 branches. School libraries often face the same kind of staffing limitations with one library media specialist responsible for several library media centers and daily work done by aides.

I would like to acknowledge the help several people provided in preparation of the book. Margie E. Herron, Director of Field Services at the South Carolina State Library, provided much editing assistance on the original handbook. Jane Ann McGregor critiqued the original version while at the Florence County Library in Florence, South Carolina. Now at the South Carolina State Library, she has made suggestions for this manuscript and offered support and encouragement. Millicent Gardner, my sister-in-law and a children's librarian just reentering the work force, encouraged me by telling me repeatedly how useful the book was to her. Mae Benne, to whom this book is dedicated, introduced me to the world of children's librarianship at the University of Washington, and her dedication to the profession, commitment to quality service, and concern for children have been a continuing inspiration to me. Last, but not least, my husband, Ken Connor, encouraged me to undertake this project and has supported my efforts to complete it.

Photo Credits

The author wishes to thank the following for allowing her to take photographs:

Chopstick Theater, Charleston, South Carolina (photo of drama group)

Dallas Dancy Child Development Center, Columbia, South Carolina (photo of visit to day care center)

Free Library of Philadelphia, Northwest Regional Branch (photo of dragon)

Kershaw County Library, Camden, South Carolina (photos of children using BookBrain software, puppets)

Richland County Public Library, Columbia, South Carolina (photos of toddler story time, storytelling festival, visit to day care center)

Zion Lutheran School, Corvallis, Oregon (photo of girls reading, boys at card catalog)

The Roles and Responsibilities of the Children's Librarian

Imagine a career where you can influence the future of the world by helping today's children develop their intellect, imagination, knowledge and values as well as visions of their own and the world's future. Imagine a career where you can help children develop a zest for learning, a lifelong love of reading, and the skills to find the answers in their quest for knowledge. Imagine a career which can help people to exercise their right to information and knowledge. Imagine a career which can help people become masters of information rather than people who are overwhelmed or controlled by information overload.

Librarians working with children in public libraries and school library media centers can do all of these things. To be successful they need to be committed to bringing children and materials together in the face of obstacles and frustrations. They need to be willing to work to make a difference in the lives of children. The opportunity to work with and influence children is a special privilege not always recognized in contemporary society. Children may be small and without much power, but the way they are taught and encouraged as children helps form their adult values and abilities. Children are the future of the world, and having a positive impact on them is one sure way to influence the future. The privilege of influencing children is not a right to mold them in our vision but to provide them opportunities to develop their own visions. Libraries as repositories of information and the imaginary visions of authors and thinkers past and present are a natural resource for children to use in learning and in refining their views of the world and the future.

Librarians working with children must like and respect children as individuals. All children are not alike and all children are not equally likeable, but librarians must be able to relate to a child's eye view of the world without looking down or talking down to the children. Children are special in many ways. Their interests and opinions are not solidified. They are curious and still are excited by new experiences and are eager to learn. However, this excitement is fragile and can be easily crushed by negative learning experiences.

Librarians working with children have the opportunity to introduce children to the joy of reading and the pleasure of books. They can introduce children to their literary heritage, the literary present, and the literary future as well as to resources to answer their questions. To get the right book to the right child at the right time is a true reflection of the librarians' task. Today, librarians also encourage children to use music, spoken words, pictures and a variety of visual and aural experiences through recordings, film, videotape, and other media.

Librarians also have the opportunity to introduce children to ways of gathering information and finding answers. These skills are increasingly important because the quantity of information available is multiplying at a phenomenal rate. Librarians need to believe that books and information can have a positive impact on children's lives. They must want every child to have the opportunity to use the library and learn from its resources. They must believe that every child has the right to information.

Librarians must be able to create an exciting, non-threatening atmosphere that will encourage children to become active library users. They must be able to promote the library and its resources in positive ways, not only to children but to parents, teachers, and other adults on whom children are often dependent for access.

Being a children's librarian requires commitment and dedication that goes beyond the hours spent at work. Often reading children's books and parts of program preparation such as learning stories has to be done away from the library. Librarians need to keep up with what is happening in the community and the world that affects children and families. It is not a profession for everyone, but for those with a vision for children and a desire to introduce them to all types of knowledge it is an exciting and challenging career.

QUALITIES OF EFFECTIVE CHILDREN'S LIBRARIANS

Liking children and books will not in themselves make a person an effective children's librarian. Certainly, children's librarians must enjoy children, understand them, and know how to direct their energies in positive ways. They also need to know children's literature well, appreciate a wide variety of styles of writing and art, know how to evaluate books and nonprint materials, and, most important, know how to bring children and books together. This takes a combination of training and experience.

Ideally, librarians working with children should have a master's degree in library science with a specialty in children's services or school librarianship. They should have courses in child growth and development. School library media specialists should meet state certification requirements. However, this standard is not always used, particularly in smaller libraries or in situations where trained personnel are not available. School districts may transfer a teacher to the library, and public libraries sometimes assign someone to children's services. In situations where a person is hired without previous background in children's literature and library service, the individual should take classes or otherwise plan a program for developing a solid knowledge of children's materials, child development, and children's services in libraries.

Librarians working with children need to have good management skills and know how to budget, plan, and evaluate services. They need to know how to promote and advance library services to children. They also need to know how to plan and do programs and activities that interest and attract children. School library media specialists, in particular, must be able to teach library skills in creative, interesting ways. Librarians working with children need to have basic programming skills such as being able to read to children effectively. Librarians who also have skills in storytelling, puppetry, art, music, drama, or crafts can use these to enrich and expand library activities. Good children's librarians will continue to develop programming skills and will round out their skills with individuals and groups in the community who can provide special activities. A good children's librarian has all of these qualities and skills. A person who can do great programs but doesn't read children's books or who can't supervise or manage a department may attract a lot of children to programs but won't provide good all-around library service. Likewise a person who knows the collection and provides good help to users, but sees no need to go beyond this won't help the library grow and develop.

VARYING ROLES AND RESPONSIBILITIES

The skills needed by librarians working with children in both school and public libraries have been analyzed and identified by the appropriate divisions of the American Library Association. In "Information Power: Guidelines for School Library Media Programs" (1988), the American Association of School Librarians lists guidelines for the education and certification of professional library personnel in the areas of library and information science, education, communications theory, and technology. In 1989, the Association for Library Service to Children adopted "Competencies for Librarians Serving Children in Public Libraries" which defines the roles and responsibilities of the children's librarian in the areas of knowledge of client group; administration and management; communication; materials and collection development; programming; advocacy, public relations, and networking;

and professionalism and professional development. These documents represent an attempt to delineate the various roles of librarians working with children and to show that these responsibilities are varied and far reaching.

SAMPLE JOB DESCRIPTION: Children's Services Librarian

General Statement of Duties

Under general supervision of the Library Director, plans, organizes, and maintains the library's children's collection; develops and implements a wide variety of children's programs; provides reference and reader's advisory service to children and parents.

Minimum Qualifications

Master's degree in Library Science from an ALA-accredited program required; specialized course work in children's services preferred; two years experience in children's services preferred.

Job Responsibilities and Examples of Services Performed

1. Assists children in use of the library and its resources
2. Assists parents and other adults in selecting appropriate children's materials
3. Reads reviews and selects books, periodicals, and nonprint materials for purchase by the children's department
4. Maintains the children's collection by regular examination and periodic weeding
5. Schedules, plans, conducts, and publicizes library activities and programs for children
6. Prepares annual department budget
7. Maintains statistical records of department use and program attendance
8. Prepares regular reports for library director
9. Maintains a pleasant, inviting environment in children's area
10. Conducts group tours and bibliographic instruction as needed
11. Cooperates as a team member with all library staff in performing any professional or nonprofessional duty essential to the achievement of efficient library operations

Essential Knowledge, Skills, and Abilities

Extensive knowledge of current trends in library service to children; ability to work with children of varied backgrounds; knowledge of materials for children; ability to supervise others and to work with all members of library staff. Must be self motivated and able to exercise initiative and independent judgment; ability to speak and write effectively.

The children's department of the public library may include one or several staff members, or it may be one of many responsibilities of one person. Children's librarians may work in one location, or they may move around a system to work in several libraries. In many small and medium-sized public library systems, there is only one person assigned part time or full time to children's services in the system. In smaller libraries and branches, children's services may just be one of many hats worn by the librarian or may be shared among staff. In larger libraries, there may be several librarians and assistants in the children's department, branch children's librarians, and also a children's coordinator who supervises or advises staff throughout the system. Some public libraries choose to hire more librarians as generalists who share responsibility for age level and other special services.

The same variety of patterns can be found in school libraries. Staff may be called school librarians or library media specialists. In a library media center there may be one or more media specialists and/or aides. Alternatively, a library media specialist may be responsible for more than one media center, or the media center may be staffed part time by a teacher or other school employees. In some districts, library media specialists may be completely on their own and be responsible for all functions of the library including acquisitions and processing. In other cases, there may be a district library media coordinator and/or processing center.

Clearly, some of these staffing patterns are more desirable than others. Much as it may be desirable to have trained, well-qualified librarians in every school and public library, this is not always the reality. Many people are accomplishing a lot for children with remarkably little staff or resources. Doing everything discussed here may not be possible in situations where staff is performing multiple responsibilities without adequate support. In other situations, the responsibilities discussed may be divided among staff.

Children's librarians or library media specialists are responsible for planning library services for children. They need to develop short- and long-term goals and objectives and plan activities to meet them. They must regularly examine and evaluate services to balance the time and emphasis given to various services and age groups served. This planning and evaluation is the foundation for developing services, and yet it is an area which is frequently neglected in the press to complete on-going routines and activities. However, planning allows librarians continuously to revise and improve services to children and to eliminate that which is no longer necessary.

SAMPLE JOB DESCRIPTION:
School Library Media Specialist

General Statement of Duties

Responsible for the daily operation and supervision of the library media center and implementation of all programs and services needed to allow students and teachers to maximize use of available resources.

Job Responsibilities

1. Selects, acquires, and processes print and nonprint materials and maintains collections as needed
2. Provides assistance to students and teachers in reference and information inquiries, finding reading and other materials for assignments and recreational use
3. Serves as resource consultant to teachers for classroom planning and prepares bibliographies and supplies materials as needed by teachers
4. Serves on curriculum planning committees
5. Develops circulation policies and procedures and supervises daily circulation routines
6. Promotes media center by use of displays, exhibits, and an ongoing public relations program
7. Supervises and trains other staff including library aides, student and other volunteers
8. Develops and implements long- and short-range plans and establishes goals and objectives
9. Prepares regular reports for principal
10. Prepares and implements annual budgets
11. Supervises annual inventory of all material
12. Provides equipment and materials for use and production of media

Terms of Employment

Salary and work year based on current district salary schedules and contract.

Evaluation

Performance will be evaluated by principal in accordance with provisions of the Board's policy on evaluation of professional personnel.

Developing and maintaining the collection is another responsibility. This is often described as book selection, but it is more than choosing books and other materials. Librarians must continuously analyze the collection to determine its needs as a basis for selection of materials. They also must withdraw materials that are no longer useful. A library's collection is the basis for its services, and developing a quality collection takes regular and consistent time and effort.

It is also important that the children's area be staffed to answer the needs of the individual child because a great collection is worthless if children do not get the help they need to use it well. In libraries where one person is responsible for system-wide service or more than one library and must of necessity be in different buildings and locations, other staff should develop a basic knowledge of children's books. The children's librarian should try to be available during peak use.

Librarians working with children are reference librarians and reader's advisors for children and for adults, including teachers and parents who use the children's area of the library or the media center. They suggest books for reading based on their knowledge of children's literature and the children. This requires getting to know the collection by reading and careful examination. They also prepare booklists and bibliographies to promote use of the collection. They help children find answers to questions or materials for school assignments or for personal interest. As part of this they teach children how to use the library. This is generally done informally on a one-to-one basis in public libraries. For school library media specialists, teaching library skills is a major part of their responsibility.

Programming for children helps make the library come alive, and librarians are responsible for planning and conducting programs for children which will help them experience both literature and the library in a positive way.

In order to promote the library's services for children, librarians must plan and execute a good program of public relations and publicity. This includes announcing and publicizing specific activities, services, and programs and also making the public, other community agencies, and, in the case of the library media center, the school, aware of services and what they can expect from the library. Generally this includes making or supervising the making of displays and keeping the library attractive, neat, and inviting.

Librarians must also promote the importance of reading to parents, teachers, and other adults working with children by talking about reading and

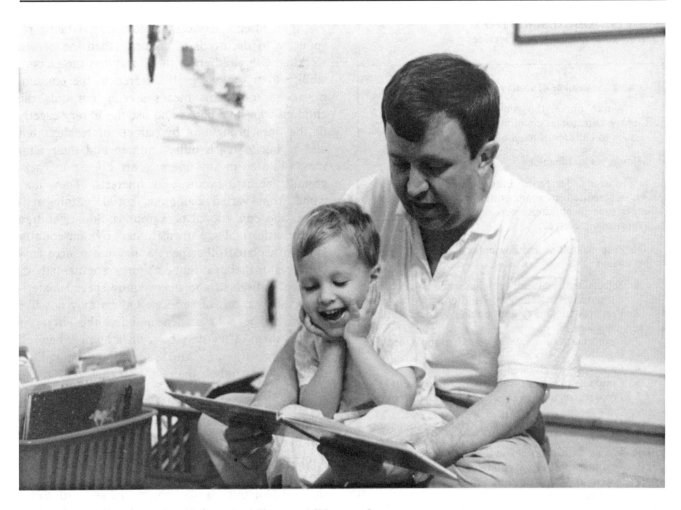

FIGURE 1. Librarians should foster reading to children at home.

the library to groups such as school faculty and community organizations.

Many children's librarians also have certain administrative or supervisory responsibilities. They must develop a budget and justifications for children's services for the administration to use in budget preparation. They monitor expenditures of department funds, compile statistics, and keep the director, principal, or supervisor as well as staff informed of activities through regular written and oral reports. Depending on the librarian's place in the staffing structure, they may be responsible for supervising services to children in a single facility or throughout a system.

Interaction with others in the community who are concerned about children results in greater awareness of the library and better community-wide services for children. Therefore, the children's librarian needs to act as a liaison to other community agencies such as schools, social services agencies, and recreation departments by keeping them informed of activities and sharing information with them about libraries. School and public librarians need to work together to promote library use and to coordinate services wherever possible. Finally, children's librarians need to act as advocates for children within the library and the community. In public libraries they need to help other staff understand children's needs. They need to ensure that library practices and procedures do not present unnecessary barriers to children. Within the community they need to keep informed about community services and resources for children and issues involving children and families.

Each public library should have job descriptions outlining the responsibilities of the children's librarians and other staff in the children's department. School districts should have job descriptions for school librarians. They provide a basis for planning and activities and are a tool for staff evaluation, and ensure that all necessary functions are someone's specific responsibility.

SAMPLE JOB DESCRIPTION:
Coordinator of Children's Services

General Statement of Duties

Works under the general supervision of the Library Director in planning and supervising library service to children throughout the library system.

Minimum Qualifications

Master's degree in Library Science from an ALA-accredited program; three years professional experience in children's services; some supervisory experience preferred.

Job Responsibilities and Examples of Services Performed

1. Selects materials for purchase and supervises all materials selection for children
2. Prepares brochures and publicity about children's services
3. Coordinates all program planning and scheduling
4. Supervises all children's services staff
5. Conducts in-service training for library staff
6. Prepares regular reports for director on children's services
7. Maintains children's collections throughout system
8. Works with branches and bookmobiles on developing services for children
9. Serves as liaison to other community agencies serving children
10. Conducts programs for children and parents
11. Prepares budget for children's services

Essential Knowledge, Skills, and Abilities

Extensive knowledge of current trends in library service to children; knowledge of children's literature and materials; programming skills; ability to work with others and to supervise and motivate staff. Must be self motivated and be able to exercise independent judgment; ability to speak and write effectively.

With the various time-consuming tasks required of a children's librarian, it is easy to lose sight of the primary focus, which is the child. Pauline Wilson of the University of Tennessee Graduate School of Library and Information Science has suggested that many children's librarians become overly immersed in children's literature to the point that their primary interest becomes books rather than serving children. She reminds librarians working with children that their focus should be on helping children grow and develop and that library materials and activities are a tool to that end. (*School Library Journal*, 1979).

If children's services are focused on being responsive to the needs of children, then the person working with children in the library has the responsibility to try to serve all children in the community or school. This means serving not only the children who love books and use the library eagerly or the ones brought in by parents or teachers but also trying to reach other children and their families. Children in any one area are diverse in background, ability, needs, and interests. They may come from varied economic, social, ethnic, religious, and educational backgrounds. Some children live in cities or large towns; others live on country lanes so isolated other people may not realize anyone lives in the area. Some children are mentally or physically disabled and may require special materials or adaptations of services. Others may not like to read or be poor readers and feel the library is not for them. They may be from a home where all entertainment is on a square screen and know little about reading other than as a school skill to be mastered.

It is a great challenge for the children's librarian to try to address these varied needs and help all children learn about the library as a source for information, recreation, education, and personal growth and development. It is an important responsibility. Not only is the library valuable to children's development, but attitudes about and experiences with the library will help determine their feelings about and support for libraries as an adult.

The roles and responsibilities of the children's librarian are varied and demanding. The key to a successful children's department is an individual who understands the diversity of these responsibilities and who can juggle the many demands and do the wide variety of tasks assigned while keeping focused on the children.

BIBLIOGRAPHY

The titles listed here are about children's services in public libraries and school library media centers in general or areas not covered more specifically in other sections of the book. Bibliographies on specific aspects of services are found at the end of the appropriate chapter.

Anderson, Dorothy J. "From Idealism to Realism: Library Directors and Children's Services." *Library Trends* 35 (Winter 1987): 393-412.

American Association of School Librarians and Association for Educational Communications and Technology. *Information Power: Guidelines for School Library Media Programs.* Chicago: American Library Association, 1988.

Association for Library Services to Children. "Competencies for Librarians Serving Children in Public Libraries." *Journal of Youth Services in Libraries* 2 (Spring 1989): 219-223.

Baker, D. Phillip. *The Library Media Program and the School.* Littleton, CO: Libraries Unlimited, 1984.

Baskin, Barbara and Karen Harris, eds. *The Special Child in the Library.* Chicago: American Library Association, 1976.

Benne, Mae. "Educational and Recreational Services of the Public Library for Children." *Library Quarterly* 48 (Oct 1978): 499-510.

Broderick, Dorothy. *Library Work with Children.* New York: H. W. Wilson, 1977.

Cleaver, Betty P. *Involving the School Library Media Specialist in Curriculum Development.* Chicago: American Library Association, 1983.

Connecticut Environments for Children Committee. *Considerations Before Writing a Public Library Building Program in Children's Services.* Hartford, CT: The Committee, 1978.
   Outlines physical needs of the children's area.

Dequin, Henry C. *Librarians Serving Disabled Children and Young People.* Littleton, CO: Libraries Unlimited, 1983.

Foster, Joan, ed. *Reader in Children's Librarianship.* Englewood, CO: Information Handling Services, 1978.

Gross, Elizabeth. *Public Library Service to Children.* Dobbs Ferry, NY: Oceana, 1967.

Haycock, Ken and Carol-Ann Haycock, eds. *Kids and Libraries; Selections from the Emergency Librarian.* Vancouver, BC: Dyad Services, 1984.

Hill, Janet. *Children Are People: The Librarian in the Community.* New York: Crowell, 1974.
   An English librarian describes taking library service out of the building and into neighborhoods.

Libraries Serving Youth: Directions for Service in the 1990's. Proceedings of a New York State Conference, April 16-18, 1986. New York: Youth Services Section, New York Library Association, 1987.

Long, Harriet. *Public Library Service to Children: Foundations and Development.* Metuchen, NJ: Scarecrow, 1969.
   A history of children's library services in the United States.

Lucas, Linda and Marilyn H. Karrenbrock. *The Disabled Child in the Library.* Littleton, CO: Libraries Unlimited, 1983.

Miller, Inabeth. *Microcomputers in School Library Media Centers.* New York: Neal-Schuman, 1984.

Nickel, Mildred. *Steps to Service: A Handbook of Procedures for the School Library Media Center.* Rev. ed. Chicago: American Library Association, 1984.

Prelude. New York: Children's Book Council, 1975 (cassettes).
   Seven sets of tapes featuring authors and authorities on using books creatively with children in schools and public libraries.

Prostano, Emanuel T. and Joyce S. Prostano. *The School Library Media Center.* Littleton, CO: Libraries Unlimited, 1987.

Public Library Association. Committee on Standards. Subcommittee on Standards for Children's Services. *Standards for Children's Services in Public Libraries.* Chicago: American Library Association, 1964.
   Although old, these were the last standards done before the American Library Association adopted the planning process and emphasized local standards.

Richardson, Selma. *Children's Services of Public Libraries.* Urbana, IL: University of Illinois Press, 1977.
   Papers from the 1977 Allerton Park Institute.

Rollock, Barbara. *Public Library Services for Children.* Hamden, CT: Library Professional Publications, 1988.

Rovenger, Judith. "Learning Differences/Library Directions: Library Service to Children with Learning Differences." *Library Trends* 35 (Winter 1987): 427-435.

Sutherland, Zena, ed. *Children in Libraries; Patterns of Access to Materials and Services in School and Public Libraries.* Chicago: University of Chicago Press, 1981.
   Essays on censorship, access, networks, the lack of interest in world patterns in children's literature, and reviewing of children's books.

Turner, Philip M. *Helping Teachers Teach: A School Library Media Specialist's Role.* Littleton, CO: Libraries Unlimited, 1985.

2008, A New Generation of Children in the Public Library. Chicago: Public Library Association, 1988 (cassette tape).
   Recording of program at the 1988 Public Library Association meeting.

Vandergrift, Kay E. and Jane Anne Hannigan. "Elementary School Library Media Centers as Essential Components of the Schooling Process: An AASL Position Paper." *School Library Media Quarterly* 14 (Summer 1986): 171-173.

Wilkins, Lee-Ruth. *Supporting K-5 Reading Instruction in the School Library Media Center.* Chicago: American Library Association, 1984.

Willett, Holly. "Current Issues in Public Library Service for Children." *Public Libraries* 24 (Winter 1985): 137-140.

Wilson, Pauline. "Children's Services in a Time of Change." *School Library Journal* (Feb 1979):23-26.

Young, Diana. "Services to Children." *Public Libraries.*
   This regular column has included many useful articles including "Library Facilities for Children" (Fall 1979), "Toddlers and Libraries" (Fall 1983), and "Evaluating Children's Services" (Spring 1984).

———. *Serving Children in Small Public Libraries.* Chicago: American Library Association, 1981. Pamphlet.

2

Understanding Children

People who work with children have the challenge and the responsibility to help them become all they can be. Young children are naturally curious and eager to learn about everything. Adults can help them retain that enthusiasm for learning and develop a desire to make a positive contribution to the world.

To work effectively with children, it is necessary to understand them and their needs. Children are not just miniature adults. They are in the process of growing and developing more rapidly than at any other time of their lives. They are affected by the people and things around them. Children enter the world of childhood at birth; they leave it for adolescence somewhere between the ages of 11 and 13. Libraries tend to define childhood by the age span they define as children's services.

For hundreds of years children in western society were thought of more as possessions than as people and were valuable for their contribution to family labor. Infants and toddlers were often left alone while parents worked. Children of the wealthy were often sent to live with a wet nurse for a couple of years and returned to their parents as strangers, only to be raised largely by servants. In the eighteenth century, a few people started to write about children as different from adults. The early Puritan settlers in America believed in a narrow, strict upbringing, but at least they realized childhood was an important period of life. While upper middle-class boys in colonial America were educated with an emphasis on the classics and rote learning, most other children received no formal education.

In the nineteenth century, children began to be seen as having special needs. Frederick Froebel founded the first kindergarten in Germany in 1857; the very name, which means child's garden, reflected a belief that children need to play and explore. In the late nineteenth century John Dewey, often known as the father of progressive education, wrote that it was important to educate the whole child. He was saying that education should touch children's emotional, social, and physical needs as well as teaching facts and information. This philosophy has been reflected in the work of the numerous educators and psychologists who have studied children and created theories of development.

Librarians working with children need to have a basic understanding of child development if they are going to be able to understand children's needs. They should have a course in child development. Because many do not, a brief overview of some of the major theories about development may be useful. No one theory has all the answers, but blending parts of each can help us understand children better.

THEORIES OF CHILD DEVELOPMENT

While Sigmund Freud's name is well known, his theory of child development based on a series of psychosexual stages is not as highly regarded today as it once was. Freud believed that children's personalities develop through a co-mingling of the id, the desire for pleasure; the superego, the conscience imposed by family and society; and the ego, the reasoning part of personality. The ego enables children to find socially acceptable ways to satisfy desire. For example, children may become tired of a story and want to throw the book on the floor, but learn instead to say that they don't want to hear it anymore. He believed that failure to resolve the conflicts in oral, anal (toilet training), and phallic (interest in sexual organs) stages during the preschool years would result in an unhealthy adult personality.

Erik Erikson was influenced by Freud. He saw life as a series of eight stages of psychosocial development which must be resolved successfully for healthy personality development. The first four stages occur in childhood. Infants from birth to eighteen months are learning basic trust or mistrust. If babies learn that mommy and daddy are loving and dependable, they have the basis for trusting other people. From eighteen months to three years they are resolving autonomy versus shame or doubt about themselves. "No!" is often toddlers' favorite word, but this is their way of asserting they are separate people with their own desires. If they don't learn that it is all right to have different wishes or ideas than other people, Erikson believed they would always be ashamed or doubtful of their own feelings. Children from ages three to five are resolving initiative versus guilt by learning to initiate actions and activities and to be responsible for their decisions. Failure to do so results in guilt feelings about doing or thinking differently. Children in this stage need opportunities to make their own decisions. From six to eleven, children are in the stage of industry versus inferiority in which they learn to either feel good about their choices and activities or to feel they are inadequate. Notice that this stage coincides with elementary school where children all too quickly sense whether they are successes or failures in school. Children who successfully pass through these stages are on their way to successful adulthood; others are more likely to grow up with personality problems and poor self concept.

John Watson, B.F. Skinner, and Albert Bandura are three representatives of a school of thought called behaviorism. They believe behavior and development are learned from the environment through conditioning and observation. Children will change behavior based on positive or negative reinforcement and punishment. For example, children will often misbehave in order to get attention; if it results in attention, even if it is negative or punitive, the attention serves to reinforce bad behavior. Behavior modification is a technique that makes use of positive reinforcement and ignoring negative behavior to change behavior. Behaviorism

has been widely used as a basis for teacher methodology and discipline in American schools. Children are encouraged to succeed for outside reinforcement in terms of grades and praise rather than for the pleasure and rewards of learning. Bandura believed children learn most through observation of parents, other adults, and peers, and that positive role models were important for positive development.

Jean Piaget focused primarily on the children's intellectual or cognitive development. His work has been very influential in early childhood education. His theory proposes that children pass through four developmental stages, each of which is a necessary foundation for the next. In the sensory-motor stage, infants learn by exploring with the senses and body movement. They learn that certain actions have distinct effects on their environment. For example, a smile brings a special response from parents. They learn that an object continues to exist when they can't see it. At about two years, children enter the preoperational stage. These children are active learners with play being the major vehicle for learning. Piaget believed children learned best through concrete experiences, which means through hands-on manipulation, and through experience with objects and people. Language develops out of concrete experiences because children cannot talk about what they have not experienced. Children at this age cannot understand abstract concepts. Instead they learn through experience. They add to their knowledge through a process of assimilation, or adding new information to what they know, and accommodation, or changing their understanding to accommodate new information. For example, a child might believe all four-legged creatures are cats. When the child realizes there are also dogs and other four-legged animals, she changes her previous understanding to accommodate new animals. As she learns to recognize more and more animals, she adds them to her understanding of animals through assimilation.

Preoperational children are egocentric, meaning that they see the world only from their own viewpoint, which is why they find it difficult to share and often seem unwilling to consider others. They see things in a linear way and cannot reverse their thought, a process that is necessary to understand the processes of reading and writing. Until children move from this stage, usually around six or seven, into the concrete operations stage they will not learn to read or do arithmetic successfully. In working with preoperational children, it is good to make the experience as concrete as possible. Bringing in real objects relating to a story can make it more understandable, for example.

From about age seven to age eleven, children are in the stage of concrete operations. They can now reverse thought and draw deductions from concrete experiences, but they are not yet capable of abstract thought. Children at this stage can understand, for example, the meaning of love if they experience it in their daily life, but they find a concept like democracy hard to really understand. Children in this stage learn best by concrete experience, and play and active participation are still important in their learning. Acting out literature, writing their own versions of stories, puppetry, and doing activities related to stories are some ways to make literature come alive for them. At this stage, they are able to see another viewpoint and can understand rules for games and sports. They tend to see right and wrong as clear-cut without any room for shadings. In the formal operations stage beginning in adolescence, children are able to think abstractly and inductively. They can create hypotheses and logically draw conclusions from them.

In contrast to Piaget, Urie Bronfenbrenner sees each child as part of a system of interconnecting parts. For the system to work successfully, all its parts must be positively connected. The total system and all its connections is the macrosystem which includes not only the systems that directly affect the child, but also the entire society. Each child is part of several microsystems which are any setting where the child is significantly affected. Among the microsystems of a typical child are home, school, neighborhood, church, and activity organizations such as sports and scouts. He called the connections between these mesosystems. For example, the relationship between a child's home and school is a mesosystem. However, children are also affected by systems in which they are not a participant, but which affect others around them. These are exosystems such as a parent's place of work or a teacher's home, because what happens there affects people who affect them.

Basically, what Bronfenbrenner is saying is that a bad day at work for Dad can make him unhappy at home, which can carry over into the child's performance in school the next day. Children who are experiencing parental conflict or divorce can be expected to act differently in their relationships with others. However, when children feel places and people are connected positively, crises cause less disruption than when children feel isolated and alone. This may be behind the appeal of problem fiction. Children like to know other kids have made it through divorce or death and come out all right. Such books help children feel less alone or let them try out, "What if this happened to me." Bronfenbrenner believes that the lack of connections between systems is what causes many children to be alienated and stresses the importance of communities working together positively and teaching children to care about others.

HOW THEORY RELATES TO LIBRARY SERVICE

By understanding how children grow and develop, librarians can plan activities and select materials which are appropriate. Such understanding can help them interpret children's behavior and know better how to direct them in positive ways. It can help them see the library not only as a place where children come to get books and hear stories, but as a part of the community with the potential to influence children's lives in positive ways. No one theory is sufficient; they all have relevance to particular children and situations. Librarians working with children are not parents or classroom teachers and cannot try to meet all of a child's developmental and educational needs. Their job is to share literature and the power of books and information with children and to help them feel positively about libraries.

Librarians can let children know they care about them by taking time to talk and listen to them. At the same time, librarians need to be consistent in their handling of behavior. Children respond to consistency and a clear understanding of what is unacceptable.

Children need to learn to be independent and responsible. Help children to learn to use the library tools themselves. Try to make children feel responsible about materials they borrow and use.

Children learn best through concrete experiences. Plan activities that involve children as well as ones where they listen or watch. Choose stories to tell that will capture their imagination and involve them in the story. Allow them opportunities to respond to the story.

Children develop at individual rates. Don't expect all children of one age to act the same.

Plan programs or activities for an appropriate age group. Varied interests and developmental levels make it impossible to reach too wide an age range effectively at any one program.

CHILDREN IN CONTEMPORARY SOCIETY

As our society is changing, there is little question that childhood is also changing. Children are affected by television, the increasing number of single-parent families, the increasing number of families with both parents working out of the home, increased mobility, the technological revolution, child abuse, and exposure to drugs and alcohol, violence, and other "adult" subjects. Whether these have positive, negative, or neutral effects on children is a matter of conjecture and divided opinions. However, it is important for librarians to examine these societal changes because they affect children's access to and use of libraries.

Perhaps the most significant change affecting children's use of libraries is the changes in family structure. The traditional stereotype of the typical American family with father as wage earner and mother working in the home is now true for only about 10 percent of American families. Families headed by a single parent or with both parents working outside the home are the overwhelming majority. One half of mothers with children ages three to five now work outside the home and this figure is increasing every year. Two thirds of working women are either sole wage earners or have husbands earning less than $15,000 a year, showing that working for many is not a career choice but an economic necessity. Over 12 million children live in female-headed households, and over half of these children are poor (*American Children in Poverty*, 1984). In Black and Hispanic female-headed households, over 70 percent of the children are poor. In fact while eight of ten white children live in two-parent households, only four of ten black children do. One of four black children lives with a parent who has never married. One half of our children will spend part of their childhood in a single-parent household (*Black and White Children in America*, 1985).

The implications of this on public library children's services are significant. Much programming and, often, library hours are based on parents being free to bring the child to the library during daytime hours. In many libraries today, it is difficult to get enough children to a preschool story hour or after-school activity because the parent is working and the child is in child care or without transportation. School-age children are also more likely to be in day care, day camp, or other programs after school or in the summer months. Public libraries must examine new ways to reach children and families and to work with those who are caring for children during the day. Libraries must encourage child care centers to come to the library or they must go out to the children in child care facilities. The family in which both parents are working or in which there is only one parent also finds time at a premium. Such parents may find less time to read to their children or to bring them to the public library. Libraries need to examine hours to ensure they are available to families when families can use them. School libraries need to have sufficient flexible scheduling to allow children to use the library for research and other assignments since it may be more difficult for many children to get to other libraries. As some schools begin after-school programs for children, the library may need to be involved in offering some special activities, programs, and other library services.

Another significant change in the lives of American children is the influence of electronic media, especially television. Children who watch excessive amounts of television have neither the time nor, frequently, the interest in other activities including the leisurely pace and greater mental demands of reading. Statistics show that the average American child spends 30 hours a week—one third of waking hours—in front of the television. That is over 1,500 hours a year. By the time many children enter school, they have watched more hours of television than they will spend in school over the next 12 years. Children raised in front of a television screen may expect flashy, sophisticated entertainment and may be less attracted to traditional library activities.

Children are greatly influenced by what they see and hear. Their heroes and heroines are often television or recording stars or cartoon superheroes rather than people who have made significant contributions to our society. For many children, in fact, television plays a bigger role in determining values than parents, school, or church or synagogue. Many experts feel that as poor or mediocre or inappropriate for children as most television programming is, its real harm is that it keeps children from doing other things such as active play, talking, and reading. Because of television, children often have less time and inclination to read. They are also likely to have shorter attention spans and to want more action-filled, fast-moving stories rather than more leisurely paced books.

If schools and libraries are to compete with television, they must find ways to make reading exciting and to use the electronic media in positive, creative ways. They must introduce children to high-quality media not available on television. Rather than ignoring television, they need to use it as a springboard to books and library activities. They must also work to help parents realize the importance of limiting television viewing.

Television has also played a role in the growth of a consumer society. Children have always wanted to have things their friends have, but the pressure to have the right toy or clothes is increased by television advertising. Television characters spawn books of questionable quality, toys, clothes, videotapes, and other items using a marketing strategy to create demand based on familiarity. Libraries must decide how their selection will be influenced by the demand for this type of literature. They should also examine how they can help children develop the skills to examine advertising and programming critically.

At the same time, television has made children more aware of the world at large and of current events. Libraries need to capitalize on what is going on and tie library activities and services into this. Television has had a role in lowering the age libraries designate for young adult services. Children seem to be growing up faster and want to put away childish things at an earlier age.

Another factor limiting children's use of libraries is parents who either cannot read or do not value reading. Parents who are illiterate cannot read to their children or assist them with their reading. Children who do not receive parent reinforcement are more likely to have reading difficulties. These parents often want to conceal their illiteracy and avoid places such as libraries where they are confronted with the written word. There is also a growing number of illiterate people who can read but don't. Adults are often as attached to television, video games, and other electronic entertainment as children, and in not reading themselves, fail to provide an example for their children.

Public and school libraries are affected by society's structures and changes. Librarians working with children need to be aware of children in a holistic sense to be able to plan and develop strategies to reach them. It is important to read about children and what affects them as well as to read books for children. Librarians also need to be aware of characteristics of children and families in their own communities. Librarians will want to learn about the community's economic and educational makeup; racial, ethnic, and cultural backgrounds; and other relevant statistical information. Community-planning agencies can frequently supply current information and future projections. By becoming knowledgeable about children in the service area, librarians will be able to do a better job planning services and programs that will interest and meet the needs of the children and parents they serve.

BIBLIOGRAPHY

American Children in Poverty. Washington, DC: Children's Defense Fund, 1984.

Black and White Children in America: Key Facts. Washington, DC: Children's Defense Fund, 1985.

Brazelton, T. Berry. *Working and Caring.* Reading, MA: Addison-Wesley, 1985.

Bronfenbrenner, Urie. *The Ecology of Human Development.* Cambridge, MA: Harvard University Press, 1979.

DeLone, Richard. *Small Futures: Children, Inequality and the Limits of Liberal Reform.* New York: Harcourt, 1979.

Elkind, David. *The Child and Society: Essays in Applied Child Development.* New York: Oxford University Press, 1979.

———. *Children and Adolescents: Interpretive Essays on Jean Piaget.* New York: Oxford University Press, 1970.

———. *The Hurried Child.* Reading, MA: Addison-Wesley, 1981.

Fraiberg, Selma. *The Magic Years: Understanding and Handling the Problems of Early Childhood.* New York: Scribner, 1959.

Goelman, Hillel, Antoinette Oberg, and Frank Smith, eds. *University of Victoria Symposium on Children's Response to a Literate Environment: Literacy Before Schooling. Awakening to Literacy.* Exeter, NH: Heinemann, 1984.
  Research on the effects of early exposure to books.

Hale-Benson, Janice E. *Black Children: Their Roots, Culture, and Learning Styles.* Rev. ed. Baltimore, MD: Johns Hopkins University Press, 1982.

Locke, Jill L. and Margaret Mary Kimmel. "Children of the Information Age: Changes and Challenges." *Library Trends* 35 (Winter 1987): 353-368.

Moody, Kate. *Growing Up on Television: The TV Effect.* New York: Times Books, 1980.

Packard, Vance. *Our Endangered Children.* New York: Pantheon, 1983.

Pogrebin, Letty Cottin. "Do Americans Hate Children?" *MS Magazine* 12 (November 1983): 47-50.

Postman, Neil. *The Disappearance of Childhood.* New York: Delacorte, 1982.

Scheffler, Hannah Nuba. *Resources for Early Childhood; An Annotated Bibliography and Guide for Educators, Librarians, Health Care Professionals, and Parents.* New York: Garland, 1983.
   Essays and bibliographies on topics from child development to art and drama activities for young children.

Wallerstein, Judith S. and Joan Bertin Kelly. *Surviving the Breakup: How Children and Parents Cope with Divorce.* New York: Basic Books, 1980.

White, Burton L. *The First Three Years of Life.* Rev. ed. New York: Prentice-Hall, 1985.

Winn, Marie. *The Plug-In Drug.* Rev. ed. New York: Penguin, 1985.

Planning for Collection Development

The materials collection is the heart of a library. Great programs, excellent publicity and public relations, good relationships with teachers, and a beautiful facility mean little if the library does not have a collection to meet the needs and wants of the people it serves.

Materials collections for children, while they have some unique features, need to be as up-to-date in both appearance and content as collections for adults. Children have the same needs for current, accurate information, and a wide variety of inviting recreational materials. The children's collection in both public and school libraries will include books for a variety of ages and reading levels as well as nonprint materials such as records or cassette tapes, filmstrips, films, videotapes, or computer programs.

Providing quality material for an attractive and useful collection on a limited budget is a challenge. Careful and continued planning and budgeting is essential if librarians are to do a good job of collection development.

Collection development is the term used to describe all aspects of collection work including selection, duplication, maintenance, and withdrawal of dated, worn, or unneeded material, and acceptance or rejection of gift materials. The word development implies a planned approach to building the collection: analyzing it for weak areas, checking it against standardized lists, monitoring use, and replacing worn and outdated items, as well as choosing and ordering new books.

Collection development is a continuing challenge for any librarian who must strive to strike the proper balance of various topics, types of materials, and reading levels as well as balancing materials chosen for popularity against those chosen for recognizable quality.

Children's collections are different from adult collections. The children's department or school library media center serves children with a wide variety of ages, interest levels, and reading abilities. For the public library this ranges from infants and toddlers touching, looking, and listening to books for the first time and older elementary to middle school children who are capable of reading just about anything in the entire library. For the school library media center, it means materials suitable for the entire age range of the school population. The collection must provide books on different reading levels as well as several books on the same subject at different reading levels. Multiple copies of popular titles are also desirable. Adult collections in public libraries, especially fiction collections, are shaped quite heavily by the demands of best seller lists, media interviews, and tie-ins. Children tend to make fewer specific demands for the latest title and to be less set about what they are willing to read although they often want more books by the same author or books about a television character.

BALANCING QUALITY AND DEMAND

Most librarians working with children attempt to expose children to good books and encourage them to broaden their reading interests. In recent years this traditional philosophy of selection has been challenged by librarians who say that libraries should purchase more mass market books, television and movie tie-ins, and other books which traditionally might not find a place on library shelves because they do not meet quality selection criteria. Librarians must develop their own philosophy about balancing quality and popularity in the collection. Following are some points to consider in determining that proper balance.

Adults read horizontally, but children read vertically. This means that most adults read on essentially the same reading level all of their adult lives. Children, on the other hand, move to books of increasing difficulty as skills grow. Children may only have a year or two when they are the right age to enjoy certain books: what is missed at that time can never be enjoyed in the same way later. Children who spend all their reading time on mediocre books may miss reading some of the best books for children. If libraries do not purchase new copies of standard titles and high-quality new books, most children will never have the opportunity to see them. Many bookstores carry only best sellers and mass market books. Many communities don't even have a bookstore.

While it is important to meet user demand, librarians must decide if it is desirable to create demand for poor quality material. Children will request titles featuring a television character or from a well-known series of books because of their comfortable familiarity. Therefore, in adding some of these books, libraries create demand for more. Children are always drawn to the familiar cartoon character or the slick bright covers, but these are not necessarily what, in the long run, they enjoy most. Just as the toy with big appeal on Christmas morning may later be ignored in favor of a more interesting one, slick books may have only short-term appeal.

On the other hand, children will ask for books which are given a lot of advertising or are related to television programs. If the library does not have some of these, some children may leave empty-handed. Isn't it better for a child to be reading something than nothing at all?

Children's books that are based on eye appeal and low cost and are designed to be sold in grocery stores, discount stores, and bookstores are known as mass market books. They are generally lower in price than other trade books because of the quantities sold, and they frequently have cardboard bindings which are not very sturdy. The quality of

text and illustration is generally not of the same standard as better trade books, but there are exceptions to this. Mass market books include series such as the *Little Golden Books*, some mystery series such as those featuring Nancy Drew and the Hardy Boys, and the teenage romance series as well as most of the books produced as television tie-ins. There are justifications to be made for including or not including these books in libraries. If purchased, be aware of their purpose and limitations, and don't overweight the collection with these books. A child seeing 50 or more Nancy Drew books on a shelf, for example, receives an unconscious message that these must be good books because the quantity makes them stand out in the collection.

There are an increasing number of television-, movie-, or toy-related books written as part of a promotional package. These books will be in demand only until the character is forgotten for the next new cartoon or superhero. Libraries may wish to spend a small amount of money to meet this temporary demand. Demand for other popular books such as stories about Curious George or Ramona will continue. If the library staff feels it is important to have some mass media, high-demand titles, they should buy only enough to meet immediate demand and recognize the books for what they are.

In an editorial in the January 1982 issue of *School Library Journal*, Lillian N. Gerhardt wrote these practical guidelines for the use of high-demand, lesser-quality books.

The Ten Commandments of Trash Novels

1. Face the fact that what is conceived for commerce is not going to be long on literary values or social consciousness, and don't work up a sweat trying to find it in books that attract the attention of financial advisors rather than critics.
2. Buy selectively and keep their percentage low in your collection.
3. Don't advertise their presence in your library collection.
4. Never feature them in book talks.
5. Keep them off your recommended reading lists.
6. Never be surprised that they are popular without your promotion.
7. Never be shocked or disheartened that your best readers read them, too.
8. Keep a handy list of the better titles among each breed and use it often.

9. Make sure your admiring award committees don't give them prizes or honors and impeach any committee that does so.
10. Remember that when the fad for any formula fiction fades, it will rise again in the next generation of readers—grin, bear it, and go on buying and promoting the best books available.

Reproduced with permission from *School Library Journal* (January 1982)/A Cahner's Magazine, R. R. Bowker Company.

Children like familiar characters. As with many adults who read only a few authors or one genre, they enjoy the security of knowing what to expect from a book. They are often reluctant to take a chance on something they may not like. Librarians need to recognize this and encourage them to try other books. Children's interests can be stimulated to include different subjects and types of stories. Helping them to broaden their interest and develop their curiosity is what education is about, and librarians are part of the educational process.

CONTROVERSIAL MATERIALS

As materials for children have broached more difficult subjects related to contemporary society, librarians have been concerned about community reactions to such things as questionable language, discusssions of sex, and portrayal of different lifestyles. Librarians need to be aware of the community as a whole, not just particular segments who may be outspoken. Librarians should avoid practicing precensorship, which means not ordering any title that might offend someone or selecting only materials that agree with their own viewpoints. Parents have full rights to control their own children's reading, listening, and viewing, but the library cannot allow a few parents to decide what is or is not appropriate for all children in the community. A clearly written, positive materials selection policy and a well-delineated procedure for dealing with questions about the collection are the best defense.

School library media centers have often felt more pressure in this area than public libraries because of the administration's desire to be responsive to parental concerns. School librarians/media specialists need to involve faculty and administrators as well as parents in developing their policies and be sure the administration supports them before a book is questioned. A parents' advisory council should also be aware of the policy. Public

libraries should make Friends of the Library groups aware of selection policies. Having a group of people who understand the reasons behind the policies can be a strong support system in case of problems.

The best foundation for a planned approach to materials selection is to have a written statement of the library's philosophy of the children's collection. Every library should have a materials selection policy that states the types of books and other materials the library will buy and not buy, standards and criteria for selection, and who is responsible for selection of materials. Although most public libraries have selection policies, a separate children's department policy can address specific department issues that may not be covered in the general policy. However, it should be consistent with the general selection policy for the library. The policy should be written and reviewed regularly by the children's librarian or library media specialist and the supervisor or principal and approved by the administrator and library or school board. A good materials selection policy will help librarians allocate the annual budget, deal with salespeople, and provide a rationale for explaining selections to anyone who may question either types of books or specific titles. Sample selection policies are provided later in this chapter.

BUDGETING FOR MATERIALS

The children's department in the public library and the school media center should be given a budget for books and other materials. In most public libraries, the children's department receives from 20 to 30 percent of the total materials budget, including that allocated for standing orders, reference books, book clubs, and any other materials. The percentage will vary depending on the juvenile percent of the population, circulation of juvenile materials, and any special collection needs. The funds of school media centers may come out of different budget areas, depending on the school district, but the media center should be given a specific budget which cannot be tapped for supplies, textbooks, or other school needs.

Children's librarians and media specialists frequently do not get involved in the budget process. In many smaller libraries, they are just informed of the amount they have to spend in the coming year. However, it is the responsibility of the children's librarian or media specialist to inform the administration early in the budget process of needs for the next year, including a justification of why the funds are needed. If the budget for the previous year was inadequate, explain why additional funds are needed. Being specific about areas of the collection which are dated and worn is more likely to bring results than a general statement that more money is needed. Put the materials budget request in writing so the director or principal has it available for budget preparation.

The budget for the year should be allocated to various areas of the collection as well as to new and replacement categories. This helps to ensure that librarians do not spend too much money in certain areas of the collection while neglecting others. It is easy to put more money into areas the librarian personally enjoys without being aware of it and a well-allocated budget helps avoid that.

In public libraries, percentages of the budget are generally allocated as follows:

Books	80-90%
Picture Books	30-40%
Fiction	20-25%
Nonfiction	35-40%
Nonprint	10-20%

In school library media centers, a greater percentage is spent on nonprint. Fewer picture books will be bought because the school is not serving young preschoolers, and the curriculum may require more emphasis on nonfiction. In all libraries, allocations will vary depending on the condition and needs of the collection. In each category, the librarian should allocate funds for specific areas. Fiction can be broken down into various genres such as mysteries, fantasy, and realistic stories; nonfiction can be broken down in subjects by the classification system. The high figure for picture books reflects the fact that in most public libraries this is the most heavily used area. Children today are reading picture books longer. They receive more wear and tear than most other books, and need to be replaced more often.

These figures are general estimates and do not account for a library's specific collection needs. By using statistical information to analyze the collection and its patterns of use over time, librarians can allocate the budget based on the specific needs of the collection and its use by the community. Decisions for allocations of funds can be made partly on past circulation figures. Under a manual

system it is cumbersome to keep circulation statistics by collection area, but most computerized systems can provide a breakdown by category of material—picture books, fiction, nonfiction by Dewey number, and type of nonprint material. This allows librarians to see exactly what materials are circulating more heavily and how patterns of use are changing, and to analyze why this is the case. Heavy use in one area may indicate a need to purchase more materials. Low use may indicate less interest, or that materials are inadequate and outdated. Using output measures, (which are discussed in Chapter 16), librarians can determine circulation rate per patron for each category of materials, and turnover rate, which shows how many times an item in one area typically circulates. Turnover rate can be very helpful in making withdrawal and replacement decisions, because librarians can determine how a particular item's use compares to the average (Hippenhammer, 1986).

Adequacy of the collection can also be analyzed by looking at its ability to meet requests. By keeping a log of requests by title and subject and whether or not they were successfully filled, librarians can identify areas that need attention in purchasing. When requests can't be filled, it should be noted whether the materials were checked out or not in the collection. Patterns of requests which can't be filled for certain titles or subjects indicates the need for duplicate copies or additional titles. Librarians can also take a particular section of the collection and analyze it for availability by comparing the shelf list or a sample to what is on the shelves at a particular point in time. If the library has a fiction title, but copies are frequently not on the shelves, this is a strong indication that duplicate copies are needed (Hippenhammer, 1986).

Statistical analysis is an important tool, but it must be used critically. Certain patterns may reflect true patterns of community interests and needs or they may reflect collection weaknesses and strengths. Without thoughtful interpretation, statistics will not in themselves provide the bases for better selection.

Analytical data help librarians to establish priorities so that they can read reviews and use bibliographies with collection objectives in mind rather than making decisions merely on whether an item is good or not.

REPLACEMENT OF MATERIALS

An important part of budget allocation is replacement of materials. In the children's area, up to half of the budget may be spent on purchasing additional copies of books in the collection because of high demand, loss, or poor condition. A library should have sufficient copies of titles so that a child has a reasonably good chance of finding what is desired in any one visit. If, for example, there is rarely more than a couple of Dr. Seuss books on the shelves, more are needed. Picture book replacement can take well over half of the budget for picture books because of high use, frequent wearing out, and the continued appeal of standard titles. Nonfiction, on the other hand, may only need 10 to 15 percent of its budget reserved for replacement since older books in many subject areas will be supplanted by new titles.

To keep the collection fresh and attractive looking, it is very important to replace worn or dirty books with clean new copies. This may mean replacing copies of very popular books every year or two. A library should aim to have standard titles look as bright and inviting as new titles. Not only is an old drab copy less likely to circulate, it also makes the entire shelf look less appealing. No one enjoys getting a book home only to find part of illustrations or text missing or pages so grimy the book is unappealing. The same is true for damaged records, tapes, toys, and other nonprint materials. Setting up a systematic schedule of replacement orders helps to ensure that lost, damaged, or worn out books are reordered. However, because books go in and out of print very rapidly, replacement has become a more difficult and time-consuming process.

Children's librarians need a schedule for ordering both new and replacement books, by specific subjects, throughout the year. The library may decide to place orders monthly or to order new books four times a year and replacement books twice a year. Certain areas of the collection may be emphasized on each order. Another approach is to plan to do replacements and updating in the collection over a one- or two-year period according to a schedule. A sample of a plan for this approach to collection development appears later in this chapter. Orders for new books should be placed in a timely fashion because they stay in print for shorter periods than previously. By monitoring how money is being spent throughout the budget year, librarians can avoid spending all the budget too early in the year leaving no money for items that are needed later. A simple chart can suffice.

Finally, it is wise to allocate less money for the last order to ensure that the budget is expended before the end of the budget year. Unexpended funds generally go into the general fund and are not carried over into the next year's budget.

However the library chooses to approach selection and collection development, it is important that it have a plan for building the collection. The library's collection is its heart and it is too important to be allowed to just happen without careful thought, study and planning.

SAMPLE:
Plan for Development of Book Collection

	Year 1	Year 2
July	Picture Books A-L	Fiction A-G
August	Picture Books M-Z	Fiction H-P
September	Classics	Fiction Q-Z
October	New Books	New Books
November	New Books	New Books
December	500-600	000-200
January	700-800	300-400
February	900, Summer Reading	Picture Books A-L
March	Biography	Picture Books M-Z
April	New Books	New Books
May	New Books	New Books

SAMPLE:
Children's Services Materials Selection Policy

The public library's objective in selecting materials for children is to make available a well-balanced collection that meets informational, recreational, and cultural needs of children from infancy through sixth grade or to age twelve.

Selection Criteria

Literature for children is an integral part of all literature. It is judged by the same standards as adult materials and is equally affected by social and political conditions. Books with deliberately discriminatory attitudes or open political and religious bias are not purchased.

Books are selected on the basis of accuracy, literary and artistic quality, quality of content, including suitability of subject matter and appropriateness of vocabulary to the reader's age, and the needs of the library collection.

Fiction is provided for a wide range of interest and reading abilities, including picture books, easy-to-read books, and stories for children. Pre-primers, primers, and other textbooks intended for school reading instruction are not purchased. Fiction for children must reveal life with integrity. Well-written books of imaginative fiction and those which authentically portray a period, incident, or way of life are selected despite the occasional use of a questionable word or illustration, provided the total impact of the book meets other basic criteria.

Nonfiction must be accurate, informative, and up-to-date, and selected in as wide a range of reading levels and interests as possible. Textbooks are purchased only when there is little or no material available in any other form on a subject. Recommended books on sex and reproduction for children are selected and shelved in their regular classified places.

Both fiction and nonfiction in series are evaluated by individual titles and must meet basic selection criteria.

Books purchased should have good quality paper, sturdy binding, and legible print. Other materials should meet quality standards for the type of material.

Magazines for children are selected on the basis of quality, potential audience, and appeal.

Nonprint materials are purchased using the same criteria as well as on visual and aural qualities.

Selection Process

The librarian in charge of children's services is responsible for the selection of children's materials. Selection for branches is done by the children's librarian in consultation with branch librarians.

Materials are selected from reputable review periodicals such as *ALA Booklist, School Library Journal, Horn Book, Bulletin of the Center for Children's Books,* and the *New York Times Book Review* as well as from bibliographies. Requests from patrons or staff will be given careful review, and selection or rejection made according to the basic criteria. Gifts are welcomed and will be evaluated according to the selection criteria before being added to the collection.

Additional copies of titles are purchased to meet demands; however, the public library cannot purchase multiple copies to meet all the demands of school reading lists.

Titles are replaced when books are lost, missing or in poor condition when the title is needed because of quality, demand, or subject content.

Weeding

Systematic weeding or withdrawal of materials is an integral part of the selection process. It is necessary to keep the collection useful and relevant. Materials are discarded because of poor physical condition, unnecessary duplication, obsolete content, and lack of use.

Controversial Materials

The library does not exclude titles, other than by budgetary limitations, except for those which do not meet selection criteria. Because there is a wide variation of criteria used by parents in determining what is suitable for their children to read, the library holds that the parent or guardian assumes final responsibility for what materials their children borrow from the library. The library attempts to judge materials on the whole and not on an isolated part. Patrons who feel that inappropriate items have been selected for the children's collection may ask for reconsideration. They will be asked to complete a "Request for Reconsideration of Library Materials" form. Requests will be reviewed by a staff committee, which will submit its recommendations to the director for recommendation to the library board.

SAMPLE:
School Library Media Center Selection Policy

The school library media center exists to serve students and faculty by implementing, enriching, and supporting the school educational program. Materials will be provided for a wide range of interests on varied levels of difficulty with diversity of appeal and representing different points of view.

Criteria for selection

Materials will be selected based on appropriateness for use with the curriculum, appropriateness in content and reading level for the intended age group, need and value to the collection, and appeal and interest to students. The quality of materials will be evaluated for clarity, adequacy of scope, validity, accuracy, objectivity, currentness, and artistic and literary quality. Materials selected must be well organized and arranged to facilitate use and include indexes, charts, maps, etc., when needed.

Selection process

The district school board is legally responsible for selection of all library materials. Responsibility for selection is delegated to the professionally trained librarians/media specialists who will consult age level and subject specialists. Teachers and students are encouraged to make recommendations.

Selection is based on reviews in reputable professional selection aids such as *School Library Journal, Booklist, Horn Book,* and bibliographies. Often nonprint materials are selected based on physical examination. Duplicate copies will be ordered only when needed. Replacement copies for lost or damaged materials will be considered on the basis of availability, need for the material, and demand.

Challenged Materials

Objections to or questions about school library media center materials should be referred to the principal. The person objecting will be requested to complete a form, "Request for Reconsideration of Library Media Center Materials." This form and the item(s) being questioned will be reviewed by the Materials Selection Committee, which will review the material and make recommendations. The principal will notify the complainant of the decision. The decision can be appealed to the district superintendent and the school board.

BIBLIOGRAPHY

Curley, Arthur and Dorothy Broderick. Building Library Collections. Metuchen, NJ: Scarecrow Press, 1985.

Evans, G. Edward. *Developing Library Collections.* Littleton, CO: Libraries Unlimited, 1979.

Gardner, Richard K. *Library Collections; Their Origin, Selection and Development.* New York: McGraw-Hill, 1981.

Gerhardt, Lillian. "The Ten Commandments of Trash Novels." *School Library Journal* 28 (Jan 1982): 5.

Hippenhammer, Craighton. "Managing Children's Library Collections through Objective Data." *Top of the News* 42 (Spring 1986): 309-313.

Kemp, Betty, ed. *School Library and Media Center Acquisitions Policies and Procedures.* 2nd ed. Phoenix, AZ: Oryx Press, 1986.

Nickelsburg, Marilyn. "Managing Youth Collections." *Public Libraries* 27 (Summer 1988): 94-96.

Spak, Karen L. "Evaluating the Children's Collection: No Easy Answers." *New Jersey Libraries* (Winter 1984): 12-17.

Book Selection

Book selection is the process of choosing books. The philosophy and care put into selection will be reflected in the library's collection. To do a good job of selection the librarian must know the collection and the community, and understand child development and the interests of children.

Children's interests vary widely. While there is a continuing high interest in dinosaurs, snakes, and crafts, children are still interested in music, physics, history, and other less requested subjects. Television, film, and other popular culture create short-term popular interests. By being alert to these, librarians can have material available when interest peaks. While librarians need to be responsive to current popular interests, it is important not to overemphasize them and to maintain a well-rounded collection.

Understanding how children grow and develop helps librarians know what children are capable of understanding or reading and what they are likely to be interested in at particular ages or stages of development. It is also important to know the children in the service area. Be aware of their backgrounds, attitudes, and interests. In urban areas, these are likely to be very diverse, but in communities within cities or in rural areas, there are likely to be some distinctive characteristics. Talk to teachers and others who work with children about what children are talking about. Be aware of reading skills as well. For example, if children in the service area tend to score lower than average on reading tests, this may affect book selection. Of course, one of the best ways to learn about what children like to read is to take time to talk with children about their reading.

Be aware of the school curriculum and recurring assignments. School librarians may find this easier to do than public librarians, since they are in the school and often involved in curriculum committees. Good communication between school and public librarians and with teachers can help all librarians anticipate demands for help with assignments. While the public library's primary purpose may not be to supply materials for assignments, children need this material, and the library has a responsibility to try to meet their needs. Children who fail to find the material needed to complete homework may be less interested in using the library for other purposes.

In addition to understanding children's interests and needs, it is also essential to know the collection that is presently in the library. Without this knowledge librarians cannot select the best of what is needed for a particular library. Even an outstanding new title on a subject may be a poor choice in a library which has good coverage on that subject and definite needs in other areas. This is a challenge for anyone new to a particular library.

In order to know collections, those who work with children must be interested in children's books and literature. Liking children cannot substitute for knowing children's books. It is important to read widely from all areas of the collection. Librarians should try to read major books, selections of popular and outstanding authors, and as many new books as possible. Where there is no children's librarian and responsibility is shared among other staff, left to one person to squeeze in among other tasks in a public library, or given to an aide in a school library, efforts should be made to gain at least a rudimentary knowledge of children's books.

A good way for a librarian to get to know a collection and to identify strengths and weaknesses is to take a standard bibliography and check the collection against it. *Children's Catalog* is a basic book list of more than 5,500 titles and includes annual supplements between editions. *Elementary School Library Collection* includes book and nonprint media. A recent edition included approximately 9,000 books and 4,000 audiovisual items. Both are arranged by Dewey number for nonfiction, fiction, and easy material and provide an annotation and approximate reading level. Both are very useful for all libraries serving children and are good examples of general bibliographies. *Junior High Catalog* is also useful for books for older children and advanced readers. Many bibliographies related to specific areas of the collection can also be useful.

To compare a library's holdings to a bibliography mark the titles that the library has either by checking the shelf list or the shelves or both. Annotations in the bibliography can be read for an idea of the book's contents. Even though checking the shelves means missing books checked out, it allows the librarian to see and touch the books. This sounds tedious, but if a small part of the collection is done at a time, it can be a good way to become familiar with the books and to become aware of what is not there that should be, especially if it is done in conjunction with more formal statistical collection analysis.

Staff should make particular efforts to examine and read new books and to regularly browse the collection. They should know what children are reading by talking to them, looking at books waiting to be shelved, and analyzing collection use. If the library has computerized circulation, it may be able to provide extensive reports on collection use and circulation of individual titles. Collection needs identified through observation, analysis, and patron requests should be noted, and books ordered as soon as possible to fill in these holes. Select books from standard bibliographies or review sources. While it is important for nonfiction to be current, the most current title may not always be the best book for the collection. Books selected from bibliographies must be checked to see if they are still in print, since books go in and out of print very rapidly.

It is particularly important to be aware of standard titles that are worn and need replacing. Ide-

ally, standard titles should be in as good condition as new books so that they will be equally appealing to children, but books going out of print and budget restraints may not always make this possible. In many cases a fresh new copy of an old standard will change it from shelf sitter to a well-read title. The child population totally changes every few years, and children continue to enjoy many older titles.

SELECTING NEW BOOKS

Selecting new books can be one of the most enjoyable parts of being a children's librarian or media specialist, but it is also very demanding. Librarians must select books which are useful to the collection and also try to buy the best of what is available. This is a real challenge since in any one year almost 4,000 books for children are published in the United States. In addition, a sizable proportion of the budget will be used for replacements and multiple copies, further reducing the number of titles which may be purchased. Books, like anything else, run in cycles. There will be virtually nothing published on a subject for years and then numerous titles will appear over a couple of years. It used to be that children's librarians could wait to read a variety of reviews on several titles before making decisions. However, the high cost of publishing and the Thor decision have changed all that. Books are forced out of print more rapidly than in the past, due in large part to the 1980 Thor decision by the Internal Revenue Service that the value of items in warehouses cannot be reduced in value for tax purposes unless they are to be sold at reduced prices or scrapped. This means that book publishers have to pay higher taxes because they can no longer declare the value of inventories at way below market value. Lower deductions result in smaller print runs and quicker decisions to allow books to go out of print, which means that librarians must make purchasing decisions more rapidly than was previously necessary (Dahlin, 1980).

At least two or three of the review journals such as *Booklist, School Library Journal, Horn Book,* and *Bulletin of the Center for Children's Books* should be read. Reading several reviews of the same books will allow comparison of reviews instead of being dependent on a single opinion. Librarians will determine their preferred sources based on the speed with which reviews appear after publication, reliability, detail, consistency, and quantity of books reviewed. Some journals review only recommended books, while others include negative or not-recommended reviews. A special science review tool, either *Appraisal* or *AAAS Science Books and Films*, can also be very helpful. They include reviews by scientists and specialists, and science is an area in which many librarians, who tend to come from the humanities or liberal arts, are less able to judge for accuracy.

Publishers' catalogs are advertisements and should not be used to select books. The descriptions are designed to sell materials, not to evaluate them. They can be useful to identify titles to watch for in reviews or titles coming back into print. Even good authors write mediocre and poor books, and it is always preferable to wait for an unbiased opinion. Catalogs of remainders and sale books fall into the same category although these can be useful in obtaining hard-to-find or out-of-print books.

Larger library systems and school districts often receive review copies of books from publishers. This allows librarians to examine and review books for themselves. In some areas, a cooperative examination center allows librarians from different libraries to examine and review books before purchase. Libraries with examination programs may have review committees which compile lists of recommended titles for branches and departments. It is wonderful to be able to examine books before purchase and avoid the disappointment of books which do not match expectations from the reviews. Examining books also may allow librarians to identify books useful for their collection which were not reviewed widely or where a reviewer did not like the book. It allows librarians to see a great number of the books published each year and get a better overall picture of the scope of publishing for children.

Examination is time consuming and it does not replace reading reviews. Libraries can do an equally good job by careful use of reviews. They may also find combined book exhibits and publisher's exhibits at state and national conferences as well as bookstores useful ways to see books. Exhibits and bookstores are good places to get an overview, but they are not good places for specific selection of books because there isn't the time to thoroughly evaluate titles and it is easy to be attracted by a quick impression only. Good reviewers spend considerable time reading and thinking about the books they review and often compare them with other similar titles.

If possible, involve more than one person on the staff in reading reviews and making suggestions. School media specialists will want to consult teachers in subject areas for suggestions. Journals directed at various teaching subject areas often have useful bibliographies and reviews. In some public libraries, a single children's librarian will order books for branches and bookmobiles, but branch personnel should be encouraged to read reviews and make suggestions. In other systems, each facility does its own ordering, but orders should be coordinated. Establishing a children's book selection committee which meets regularly can be useful not only in selection but in establishing library goals and objectives for the collection.

Selection cannot be done in isolation. An outstanding new book on rocks may not be a good purchase if the collection is very strong in this area and there are other areas with definite needs. Specific priorities should be established for collection development each year. By targeting one or two areas of the collection that need improvement, money can be allocated specifically to these areas.

Annual bibliographies of outstanding books, such as the *Notable Children's Books* lists compiled by a committee of the Association for Library Service to Children of the American Library Association, *Horn Book's* "Fanfare," or *School Library Journal* and *Booklist's* lists of best books are helpful in noting quality titles that may have been missed in the selection process. These lists include books the compilers consider the best of the year after examining the year's publishing output. Most libraries purchase Newbery and Caldecott Medal books, but many pay little attention to recipients of other children's book awards, which may be equally or more suitable for a particular collection. Library periodicals list winners of such awards as the *Boston Globe-Horn Book Awards*, the Coretta Scott King Award, the Mildred L. Batchelder Award for translations, and some foreign awards such as the British Carnegie and Greenaway Medals, their counterparts to the Newbery and Caldecott medals.

Some book clubs offer special plans for libraries. Selections are often carefully made, bindings durable, and discounts substantial. A library may get some titles from a book club which it would have rejected for purchase; therefore, librarians must decide if they are willing to allocate a portion of the budget to materials that the library does not select. To evaluate book club memberships, determine the percentage of the book budget they take and the desirability of books available through the program. If the library uses book clubs, it should be careful not to order from regular sources books that will be supplied by the book club.

Beware of book salespeople who visit libraries and bring books librarians can examine. This is not a good way to purchase children's books. There is simply not enough time during a salesperson's visit to do more than give a cursory examination to see if format and illustrations are appealing. Staff cannot evaluate the quality of the writing, or the books' accuracy. Most quality publishers for children do not do their major distribution of new books through salespeople. Many of the books sold directly to libraries by children's book salespeople are poor or mediocre in quality and are published by less than the top quality publishers. Many of the books may not have been reviewed or have received less than enthusiastic evaluations. Other books are remainders, books sold off by the publisher at a very large discount to unload excess stock. Often these are books which never sold well either because of poor reviews or lack of appeal. Nonfiction may be dated. Occasionally librarians may find good titles here, but unless they really know children's books and authors well, they may be unable to distinguish these.

Salespeople also frequently handle sets of books on particular subject areas such as a special encyclopedia on science or American history. Before purchasing these, it is important to compare their coverage with general encyclopedias which may give just as good coverage of the subjects. They should also be compared with what is already in the collection on the subject. Purchase of a set on a subject may take most or all of the budget for that subject area for a smaller library or branch, so it is important to be sure it is the best expenditure of the funds. With sets of books that are not reference books, titles should be evaluated individually, because there may be wide variations in quality and accuracy.

Librarians who decide to see salespeople and examine their books should remember that it is not necessary to place an order immediately. Note books that may be worthwhile additions, and check the collection, budget, and reviews, if possible, before making final decisions. Salespeople and pub-

lishers are in business to make money. When they talk about how well written or popular the books are, remember that their goal is to make a sale. Books ordered from salespeople usually come without catalog cards or processing which can be an inconvenience if your library orders books preprocessed with catalog cards and with pockets and plastic jackets attached.

Another direct sales approach is on approval books which are sent to libraries with the assumption that once the books are there, the librarians will buy more titles from that publisher than if they selected merely from reviews. Smaller libraries, in particular, must consider if staff has time and expertise to evaluate these books adequately.

Warehouse operations also offer librarians the opportunity to order books at greatly reduced prices or to visit a warehouse and shop from the shelves. These businesses usually deal largely with remainders and present the same problems as buying from salesmen.

Ordering from reviews can sometimes be frustrating. It's difficult to make a decision based on someone else's opinion. It can also be disappointing when books do not live up to expectations. However, taken as a whole, it is the method that will likely result in better quality, more balanced collections.

BINDINGS AND FORMAT

Bindings are an additional consideration in children's book selection. Most adult titles come in a standard trade binding and perhaps in paperback. Children's books, however, are often available in a choice of bindings. Generally, they can be classified into the following types. Trade binding, the standard edition available in bookstores, can include either cloth- or paper-covered boards. The spine may be glued or sewn but not reinforced, and there is a wide variety in how sturdy the binding is. Trade books are sold at a discount to libraries. Publisher's library bindings are more durable, have washable covers, and are usually reinforced with cloth. They are generally sold at net price or with a small discount. Publisher's library bindings are almost exclusively sold to libraries. Reinforced binding is the only style now used by some publishers to avoid publishing both a trade and library edition. The discount on these varies.

Pre-binding is a method of giving a book an extra strong binding. It is generally done by a separate company which then sells the books to the libraries. The company purchases the book sheets from the publisher and puts on an extremely durable cover made of buckram or cloth reinforced with resin. The cover is reinforced to meet standards for a class A binding set by the Library Binding Institute. These are the only bindings that have a standard quality, and the covers are very durable. Libraries receive little or no discount. Their primary benefit is long wear. Because the bindings are tight, they do not lie open flat very easily. Even with picture covers, pre-bound books have an institutional look which detracts from their visual appeal. Because these books are already more expensive, some libraries do not want to spend the additional money adding plastic jackets. However, the sun will fade the buckram covers and the pictures on them which can make them look drab. Jackets greatly improve their appearance and prevent fading. Some libraries find prebound books are particularly useful for picture books where large size puts strain on bindings and where use is hard and extensive. They can also be useful with other heavily used titles. For those books where such heavy use is not anticipated, the additional cost may not be justified.

Another method of reinforcing books is used with paperbacks. Covers are impregnated with a hard durable plastic. This can give paperbacks a longer shelf life, but it does remove some of the informal, easy-to-carry feeling that helps make paperbacks so popular.

Paperbacks are used more and more in libraries because of their popularity and lower cost. In many libraries they are not catalogued and are displayed on paperback racks randomly. This encourages browsing, but makes it more difficult to find specific titles quickly. Libraries should consider using some paperbacks in their regular catalogued collection. They can provide less expensive duplication. In smaller libraries or where money is tight, they can be a way to afford quality fiction titles which the library may otherwise pass over because they are less likely to be very popular. Paperbacks can also be surprisingly durable although picture books are less so because their size and format strains the binding. Books often appear in paperback a very short time after the hardback edition. In many cases the paperback edition may

also remain in print after the hardback is out of print. There are also increasing numbers of paperback originals, titles not available in hardcover.

In deciding on format and binding, consider how much the book will be used and how soon it will be dated. A book which will most likely not be read widely or one which will be dated in a few years should be purchased in the binding which will give the best discount. Most books of this type should be purchased in trade binding to get the maximum discount or in paperback, if available. Much fiction and nonfiction fits into this category. While there is a large number of standard fiction titles which will be replaced as needed, much of the fiction collection will not be replaced. This goes against popular beliefs about the collection. However, consider how many new titles are bought each year, and of these, how many will be popular enough to wear out and need replacing. It is probably fewer titles than most librarians would think. Therefore, it may be less expensive in the long run to purchase new titles in trade editions and hope that when one needs replacing, it will be available. The same is true of much nonfiction. Picture books generally get heavier use. Not only is circulation high, but a picture book may be read numerous times during a single circulation. Again, the large size and format of many picture books puts a strain on bindings. Therefore, it may be worth the additional cost to purchase them in reinforced bindings of some type.

No matter what bindings are chosen, plastic jackets make books both more appealing and more durable. The plastic gives extra support, is washable, and gives the book a continuing new appearance. If the plastic jacket later tears, it can either be replaced or removed, leaving a clean, new-looking binding underneath.

Pre-bound editions, paperbacks, and plastic covered paperbacks may also be available after the trade hardback has gone out of print and so represent a valuable way of obtaining otherwise unavailable books. The rate at which books go out of print now makes it imperative that librarians be aware of all options for attaining books.

SELECTION CRITERIA

Children's librarians must balance what they believe children need or should be exposed to with what they perceive as children's wants and interests. Limited budgets can make it tempting to order only those items which will be popular or in demand. Not only does this assume the library will not reach beyond current users, it also devalues the interests of the children who have different interests than the majority.

Children's librarians must try to purchase materials that will meet the growing needs of a variety of children. Different children have differing levels of understanding and different problems and concerns, and come from a wide variety of home situations and cultures, all of which will affect their interests.

In selecting books, librarians should look for books which will help children to expand their minds, imaginations, curiosity, and creativity. This includes materials which explore the real and imaginary worlds of the past, present, and future, and materials which provide new information. By providing materials which introduce children to both their own and different cultures, countries, and societies, libraries can help children develop world understanding. Through materials about their own cultural heritage, children can develop self esteem and pride. Other books will help children develop their understanding of social and moral questions of good and bad, right and wrong, and other values and attitudes. By giving children the opportunity to explore as wide a range of topics as possible, librarians are providing them with the basis to dream for their future. Children also need books and other materials for simple enjoyment, however. If children are to enjoy reading, they must have things that are fun to read.

It is also necessary to expose children to the collection through displays, book talks, programs, and other activities. Children will not benefit from books on art, nature, history, or ethics if the library makes no effort to interest children in using these materials outside of school assignments.

Librarians must consider the value of the book for the collection and the quality of the book itself. There are some generally accepted qualities to look for in both fiction and nonfiction books. Good reviewers should point out these in their evaluations.

EVALUATING CHILDREN'S STORIES

In stories and fiction, the setting must be convincing. Is the time and place accurately portrayed? Does the writer convincingly evoke a feeling of life at the time and place in a way that someone can understand? Facts about the setting should be incorporated naturally into the story although, if necessary, additional background details can be provided in an introduction.

The story may be written in the first person or third person and be told by a main character or onlooker. Whatever the "voice" of the story, it should be believable and the person in the story should be in a position to know all that he or she is telling. If, for example, a child narrator knows more details about other characters than one might reasonably expect, it may not be convincing.

Characters should be realistically drawn with strengths, weaknesses, and convictions. They should grow and develop within a story, although one would expect less of this in a picture book than in a novel. They should act in ways logical for their ages and circumstances, or, if they don't, the author should provide some justification for their unusual behavior. Taken as a whole the characters should be believable and not one-dimensional or stereotypic.

The plot should develop consistently and naturally without excessive use of coincidence or outside intervention. There should be sufficient action or conflict to keep children interested. The story should have a beginning, middle, and end, and should not drag on after the climax. The best stories are original or have a fresh approach to a common situation rather than being written to a formula. The latter is a common criticism of many mysteries and junior romances, for example. Children enjoy the security of knowing what to expect, and there is a place in the collection for some less-than-original fiction, but recognize it for what it is.

The language, structure, and vocabulary should be appropriate for the story and the intended age of the reader. Dialogue should be natural, and narration and dialogue well balanced.

Abridgements and adaptations are done with the idea of making a book accessible to younger children or to make it more appealing to contemporary children. An abridgement retains the author's writing but cuts some of the text, perhaps eliminating incidents or chapters. An adaptation is

FIGURE 2. The reward of careful book selection is in seeing children enjoy library books. (Zion Lutheran School Library, Corvallis, Oregon)

a rewriting of the story, retaining the plot but not the author's words. Adaptations should be avoided because they lack the original flavor of the book. A child reading a picture book version of *Little Women*, for example, is not really reading *Little Women* at all, but only a plot condensation. Abridgements are acceptable for certain books that may be too long or difficult for children, but they should be well done.

Theme conveys the main idea or the point of the story. Even picture books for the young child can have an underlying meaning behind the story line. If the story has a distinct theme, it should be well enough developed so that children can understand what the author is trying to say. The best books are ones where children can experience something new or learn about themselves or others. However, theme is not the same as instruction or a lesson, which is better defined in literature as didacticism. Books whose overriding purpose is to teach or preach are generally dull and unexciting.

These stories are less effective than ones which weave examples of behavior and facts into a story in a way that allows readers to draw their own conclusions.

Illustration should accurately reflect the facts and atmosphere of the story. In fiction, illustration supplements and enhances the story but is not essential to its enjoyment. In picture books, illustration is as important as text. People evaluating picture books must learn to examine critically both text and illustration and how they work together. No matter how beautiful pictures are, if they don't complement the text, a picture book will not be successful.

EVALUATING ILLUSTRATION

In a picture book, text and illustration must work together to tell the story. A young child wants the pictures to tell the story, and picture book illustration is really a form of storytelling. Illustration is not like a painting that stands on its own. It is not intended to be hung on a wall. Instead it is art actively involved in telling a story. If beautiful pictures are to be successful illustrations, they should reflect what is happening in the story, show characterization, and reinforce the mood of the story. The way the artist uses line, color, design, and composition, and the style and medium of art used are important, but first the illustrations must work with the text. If they do not, the result is a series of pictures and a story that do not quite seem to fit together. Strong text and mediocre illustration or mediocre text and wonderful illustration are common in picture books. In the best picture books, text and illustration fit together so well, one can hardly imagine one without the other.

There is a wonderfully broad range of appropriate illustration for children from the simplest line drawing to complex paintings. More complex illustrations are not necessarily better. There is also not a typical style that children prefer. Illustrations which are saccharine sweet or overtly nostalgic reflect a romanticized adult perception of childhood. Those that are overly cartoon-like often represent too conscious an effort to draw what they think children like. Neither is generally very successful. At the other end of the spectrum, books which are extremely sophisticated or too adult often find a limited audience with children.

In evaluating picture book illustration one should look first for that merging of text and illustration. Facts from the story need to be accurately portrayed in the illustration. Good illustration may expand beyond the text, adding details, humor, or additional character personality, for example, but should not conflict with it. Medium and technique must be well done. Beyond the text and pictures, the format should be examined. Jacket design, endpapers, and layout are all integral to the overall impression the book makes. Wordless books should get across a story or concept clearly by the pictures alone.

In alphabet, number, and other concept books, the text often plays a much more minor role. Here it is important to judge if the pictures accurately portray and promote understanding of the concepts presented. In board books and other books for very young children where the goal is object identification rather than storytelling, pictures should clearly represent the story. There has been a tremendous growth in the number and quality of board books for infants and toddlers. The same basic criteria apply to simple board book stories, but stories and pictures should not have extraneous details. In stories for very young children, unnecessary detail and embellishment may be confusing.

EVALUATING NONFICTION

Some nonfiction books are subject to some of the same criteria as imaginative works. In evaluating a biography, for example, the characterization of the subject and portrayal of the setting are important. Poetry and folk literature must meet literary standards for setting, characterization, and other qualities. The best nonfiction books on any subject are successful as literature as well as being providers of information. They should stimulate interest and further questions about the subject.

There are, however, some special criteria to use in evaluating any nonfiction. The scope of the book should be appropriate for the target audience in terms of concept, detail, and arrangement. The information should be pulled together to create a unified book and not be a grouping of facts which are not clearly connected. The text and illustration must be accurate and current, reflecting recent knowledge or events. Facts or dialogue should not be fictionalized. While some material may need to be simplified for children, it should not be oversimplified so that it becomes inaccurate or written in a way that talks down to children. The bias or position of the author, if any, should be clear, but should not slant the text to make it misleading. The author should be qualified to write on the subject.

In nonfiction, the presence of features such as tables of contents, glossaries, and indexes are important for information retrieval and complete understanding. Suggestions for further reading are useful to the child who wants to know more. Suggested titles should be appropriate for children reading the book. Bibliographies of other materials used in writing the book give some authority to the text.

Illustrations in an informational book should be informative and not just decorative. They should help make the text clear and understandable. At the same time they should be good quality drawings or photographs. The illustrations should appear near the text to which they relate. They should be appropriate for the subject matter and illustrate important points. If maps and charts are appropriate to the subject matter they should be included and be clearly drawn, well labeled, and easily understood. There are, of course, nonfiction books which are intended to create a mood or express a viewpoint or idea rather than to provide informational fact. Illustration in these books will need to be evaluated on how it conveys the purpose of the text.

REFERENCE BOOKS

Most public libraries and school media centers have a reference section for children, which contains books for answering specific questions. Usually these books are noncirculating or have a limited circulation. A basic children's reference collection should include at the very minimum, encyclopedias, dictionaries, atlases, and almanacs designed for use by children. It should have indexes to fairy tales and children's poetry collections as well as bibliographies of children's books. Depending on library size and accessibility of a larger reference department, it may include special science or geography encyclopedias, and other special subject titles useful for answering questions. Tools beyond a general encyclopedia should be included if children's needs are to be met. It is important that reference books be regularly updated to keep them accurate.

Some smaller public libraries may have a single reference collection to serve all patrons. In this situation it is important that it include reference tools with format and reading level appropriate for children. For example, a children's dictionary and atlas would still be necessary since children might be overwhelmed at adult versions.

This basic discussion of criteria is only a starting point for book evaluation. There are numerous books devoted exclusively to evaluating and analyzing children's books. Reading books such as Rebecca J. Lukens's *A Critical Handbook of Children's Literature* (1986) and others can provide librarians with a deeper understanding of children's literature and provide them with skills that will lead to better evaluation of children's books.

BIBLIOGRAPHY

General

Dahlin, Robert. "Thor: How Hard Will the Hammer Fall?" *Publisher's Weekly* 218 (Dec 26, 1980): 28-32.

Annual Lists

"Best Books." *School Library Journal.*
Books for Children. Children's Book Center. Library of Congress. (Formerly called *Children's Books.*)
"Children's Choices." Compiled by Joint Committee of the International Reading Association and the Children's Book Council. Printed in *Reading Teacher* and in pamphlet form by the Children's Book Council.
"Children's Reviewers' Choice." *Booklist* (January).
"Fanfare." *Horn Book Magazine* (June).
Museum of Science and Industry Basic List of Children's Science Books. Comp. by Bernice Richter and Diane Wenzel. Chicago: American Library Association, 1985-.
"Notable Children's Books." Association for Library Service to Children, American Library Association. Printed in *Booklist* (early spring) and in pamphlet.
"Notable Children's Books in the Field of Social Studies." Compiled by a joint committee of the National Council for Social Studies and the Children's Book Council. Printed in *Social Education* (April) with reprints available from the Children's Book Council.
"Outstanding Science Trade Books for Children." Compiled by a joint committee of the National Science Teachers Association and the Children's Book Council. Printed in *Science and Children* (March) with reprints available from Children's Book Council.
"Science Books and Films Best Children's Science Books." *Science Books and Films* (Nov/Dec).

Bibliographies of Bibliographies

Association for Library Service to Children. *Selecting Materials for Children and Young Adults: A Bibliography of Bibliographies and Review Sources.* Chicago: American Library Association, 1980.
Ettlinger, John R. T. and Diana Spirt. *Choosing Books for Young People: A Guide to Criticism and Bibliography.* Vol 1: 1945-1975. Chicago: American Library Association, 1982. Vol 2: 1976-1984. Phoenix, AZ: Oryx Press, 1987.
Meacham, Mary. *Information Sources in Children's Literature.* Westport, CT: Greenwood Press, 1978.
Lists resources for collection building, author information and using books with children.
Quimby, Harriet and Margaret Mary Kimmel. *Building a Children's Literature Collection: A Suggested Basic Reference Collection for Academic Libraries and Suggested Basic Collection of Children's Books.* 3rd ed. Middletown, CT: Choice, 1983.

Bibliographies of Children's Books

Note: Library selection tools listed here include many that will be useful in helping patrons find books on particular topics.

Adell, Judith and Hilary Dole Klein, comps. *A Guide to Non-Sexist Children's Books*. Chicago: Academy Press, 1976.

The Afro-American in Books for Children Including Books about Africa and the West Indies: A Selected List. 3rd ed. Washington, DC: District of Columbia Public Library, Children's Services, 1985.

Archer, Marian Fuller, ed. *Reading for Young People: The Upper Midwest*. Chicago: American Library Association, 1981.

Azarnoff, Pat. *Health, Illness, and Disability; A Guide to Books for Children and Young Adults*. New York: Bowker, 1983.

Baskin, Barbara and Karen Harris. *Books for the Gifted Child*. New York: Bowker, 1980.

——. *Notes from a Different Drummer; A Guide to Juvenile Fiction Portraying the Handicapped*. New York: Bowker, 1977.

Bernstein, Joanne. *Books to Help Children Deal with Separation and Loss*. 2nd ed. New York: Bowker, 1983.

Black Impressions: A Book List for Children and Parents to Share. Baltimore, MD: Enoch Pratt Free Library, 1986.

Bracken, Jeanne, et al. *Books for Today's Young Readers*. Old Westbury, NY: Feminist Press, 1981.

Children's Catalog. 15th ed. New York: H. W. Wilson, 1986.

Cianciolo, Patricia J. *Picture Books for Children*. 2nd ed. Chicago: American Library Association, 1981.

Cuddigan, Maureen and Mary Beth Hanson. *Growing Pains: Helping Children Deal with Everyday Problems Through Reading*. Chicago: American Library Association, 1988.

Dale, Doris Cruger. *Bilingual Books in Spanish and English for Children*. Littleton, CO: Libraries Unlimited, 1985.

Dorsett, Cora Matheny. *Reading for Young People: The Mississippi Delta*. Chicago: American Library Association, 1983.

Dreyer, Sharon Spredeman. *The Bookfinder; A Guide to Children's Literature about the Needs and Problems of Youth Aged 2-15*. Circle Pines, MI: American Guidance Service, 1977; Vol. 2, 1981; Vol. 3, 1985.

Elleman, Barbara. *Popular Reading for Children; A Collection of the Booklist Columns*. Chicago: American Library Association, 1981.

——. *Popular Reading for Children II: A Collection of the Booklist Columns*. Chicago: American Library Association, 1986.

Flemming, Carolyn Sherwood and Donn Schatt. *Choices, A Core Collection for Young Reluctant Readers*. Evanston, IL: John Gordon Burke Publishers, 1983.

Friedberg, Joan Brest, June R. Mullins, and Adelaide W. Sukiennik. *Accept Me as I Am; Best Books of Juvenile Nonfiction on Impairments and Disabilities*. New York: Bowker, 1985.

Gillespie, John T. *The Elementary School Paperback Collection*. Chicago: American Library Association, 1985.

——. *The Junior High School Paperback Collection*. Chicago: American Library Association, 1985.

——. *Publishers and Distributors of Paperback Books for Young People*. Chicago: American Library Association, 1987.

Gillespie, John T. and Christine B. Gilbert. *Best Books for Children; Preschool Through the Middle Grades*. 3rd ed. New York: Bowker, 1985.

Harmon, Elva A. and Anna L. Mulligan, eds. *Reading for Young People: The Southwest*. Chicago: American Library Association, 1982.

Haviland, Virginia, et al. *The Best of Children's Books, 1964-1978*. Washington, DC: Library of Congress, 1980.

Heald, Dorothy, ed. *Reading for Young People: The Southeast*. Chicago: American Library Association, 1980.

Hinman, Dorothy and Ruth Zimmerman, eds. *Reading for Young People: The Midwest*. Chicago: American Library Association, 1979.

Laughlin, Mildred, ed. *Reading for Young People: The Rocky Mountains*. Chicago: American Library Association, 1980.

McCauley, Elfrieda B. *Reading for Young People: New England*. Chicago: American Library Association, 1985.

Meacham, Mary, ed. *Reading for Young People: The Great Plains*. Chicago: American Library Association, 1980.

——. *Reading for Young People: The Northwest*. Chicago: American Library Association, 1980.

Mertins, Barbara, ed. *Reading for Young People: Kentucky, Tennessee, West Virginia*. Chicago: American Library Association, 1985.

National Council of Teachers of English. Committee on the Elementary School Booklist. *Adventuring with Books; A Booklist for Pre-K-Grade 6*. New ed. Urbana, IL: National Council of Teachers of English, 1985.

New York Public Library Black Experience in Children's Books Committee, comp. *The Black Experience in Children's Books*. Rev. ed. New York: New York Public Library, 1989.

The Newbery and Caldecott Awards: A Complete Listing of Medal and Honor Books. Chicago: American Library Association, 1987.

O'Connell, S. M., V. J. Montenegro, and K. Wolff. *The Best Science Books and Audio-Visual Materials for Children*. Washington, DC: American Association for the Advancement of Science, 1983.

Olexer, Marycile. *Poetry Anthologies for Children and Young People*. Chicago: American Library Association, 1985.

Pearl, Patricia, comp. *Religious Books for Children: An Annotated Bibliography*. Rev. ed. Bryn Mawr, PA: Church and Synagogue Library Association, 1988.

Pennypacker, Arabelle. *Reading for Young People: The Middle Atlantic*. Chicago: American Library Association, 1980.

Peterson, Carolyn Sue and Ann Fenton. *Reference Books for Children*. Metuchen, NJ: Scarecrow Press, 1981.

Peterson, Linda Kauffman. *Newbery and Caldecott Medal and Honor Books: An Annotated Bibliography.* Boston: G. K. Hall, 1982.

Polette, Nancy and Marjorie Hamlin. *Celebrating with Books.* Metuchen, NJ: Scarecrow Press, 1977.

Reading for the Fun of It: A Guide to Books for Children with Learning Disabilities. Elmsford, NY: Westchester Library System, 1986.

Richardson, Selma. *Magazines for Children: A Guide for Parents, Teachers, and Librarians.* Chicago: American Library Association, 1983.

Sutherland, Zena, ed. *The Best in Children's Books.* Chicago: University of Chicago Press. Vol 1: 1966-1972, 1973; Vol 2: 1973-1978, 1980; Vol 3: 1979-1984, 1986.

Thomas, Virginia Coffin and Betty Davis Miller. *Children's Literature for all God's Children.* Atlanta, GA: Knox Press, 1986.

Tway, Denise, ed. *Reading Ladders for Human Relations.* 6th ed. Washington, DC: American Council on Education, 1981.

Wilkin, Binnie Tate. *Survival Themes in Fiction for Children and Young People.* Metuchen, NJ: Scarecrow Press, 1978.

Wilms, Denise Murko, ed. *Science Books for Children.* Chicago: American Library Association, 1985.

Winkel, Lois, ed. *Elementary School Library Collection.* 16th ed. Williamsport, PA: Bro-Dart, 1988.

Wynar, Christine Gehrt. *Guide to Reference Books for School Media Centers.* 3rd ed. Littleton, CO: Libraries Unlimited, 1986.

Children's Literature—Evaluation and Criticism

Bader, Barbara. *American Picture Books from Noah's Ark to the Beast Within.* New York: Macmillan, 1976.
A critical analysis of American picture book art.

Carr, Jo, comp. *Beyond Fact. Nonfiction for Children and Young People.* Chicago: American Library Association, 1981.
Essays on nonfiction and its evaluation.

Children's Book Council. *Children's Books: Awards and Prizes.* New York: Children's Book Council, 1986.

England, Claire and Adele Fasick. *Childview: Evaluating and Reviewing Materials for Children.* Littleton, CO: Libraries Unlimited, 1987.
Criteria for selecting print and nonprint.

Fisher, Margery. *Intent Upon Reading; A Critical Appraisal of Modern Fiction for Children.* New York: Watts, 1961.
Although old and heavily British, Fisher has insightful comments about each type of fiction.

————. *Aspects of Non-Fiction for Children.* New York: Crowell, 1972.
Explores the qualities of good nonfiction by comparing several books on each of several topics.

Hearne, Betsy. *Evaluating Children's Books, Prelude, Series 4.* New York: Children's Book Council, 1979 (cassette).

Lukens, Rebecca. *A Critical Handbook of Children's Literature.* 3rd ed. Glenview, IL: Scott Foresman, 1986.
Cogent discusssion of the elements involved in evaluation of children's books.

MacCann, Donnarae and Olga Richard. *The Child's First Books: A Critical Study of Pictures and Texts.* New York: H. W. Wilson, 1973.

Smith, Lillian H. *The Unreluctant Years; A Critical Approach to Children's Literature.* Chicago: American Library Association, 1953.
Old but a classic overview.

What's a Good Book. Public Library of Dayton and Montgomery County (OH), 1982 (16mm film).

Textbooks

Huck, Charlotte. *Children's Literature in the Elementary School.* 4th ed. New York: Holt, 1987.

Rudman, Masha Kahakow. *Children's Literature: An Issues Approach.* 2nd ed. New York: Longman, 1984.

Sutherland, Zena and May Hill Arbuthnot. *Children and Books.* 7th ed. Glenview, IL: Scott Foresman, 1986.

Book Review Sources

Appraisal. Children's Science Book Review Committee. Three times a year.
Each book is reviewed by a librarian and a scientist.

Booklist. American Library Association. Semimonthly.
Recommended titles only. Reviews print and nonprint.

Bulletin of the Center for Children's Books. University of Chicago Press. Monthly except August.

Horn Book Magazine. Horn Book, Inc. Bimonthy.
Recommended books only; articles on children's literature.

Interracial Books for Children Bulletin. Council on Interracial Books for Children. Eight issues a year.
Emphasizes values and socio-political viewpoints.

New York Times Book Review. Fall and spring children's book supplements and a few books reviewed weekly.

School Library Journal. Cahners Publishing. Monthly.
Includes nonprint and computer software.

Science Books and Films. American Association for the Advancement of Science. Five issues a year.

Selection of Nonprint Materials

Circulation of films, videotapes, filmstrips, records, cassettes, and even computer software is now considered a standard part of library service to children in many libraries of all sizes. While all libraries may not have all these types of materials, it is safe to say that most have at least some nonprint materials for children. Nonprint materials may be circulated like books, reserved for in-library use, or used only for programming, depending on the library's resources, equipment, and philosophy.

Nonprint materials include recordings in a variety of formats (records, cassettes, and compact discs), films, videotapes, filmstrips, computer software, and realia such as toys, puppets, and other hands-on materials. Ideally, nonprint materials should be seen as an alternative way of learning and enjoying literature, and not as a frill. In our society they are a primary way of learning and entertainment. For many children they are more familiar than books. While there are many homes without books, it is a rare home that does not have a television set except by conscious choice. A high percentage of homes also has videotape players and recording equipment. This means that libraries, if they want to enhance their role in providing information and recreation, must view nonprint materials as an integral part of the collection.

Schools have, in general, done a much better job than public libraries in giving nonprint materials a significant emphasis in the collection. In fact, many, if not most, school libraries are now called library media centers and their librarians, library media specialists, to reflect this philosophy. This greater enthusiasm for nonprint materials is at least in part due to their popularity and usefulness for classroom use.

There should be a specific budget allocation for each type of nonprint material in the collection. In times of budgetary cutbacks or restraint, nonprint materials should not be the first items cut, but should receive a reduction that parallels book budget reductions. In addition, the nonprint collection should be developed carefully, using critical selection standards, and be maintained by regular weeding and replacement. This approach treats nonprint materials as important and reflects the fact that, in contemporary society, aural and visual literacy are important skills.

Both children and adults are greatly influenced by what they hear and see on radio, television, and film as well as through the written word. They see news almost the instant it happens from all over the world. Children today are familiar with crime, violence, drug abuse, war, and a host of other contemporary issues through television. They see entertainment programs where violence is glorified. Most children look at these programs uncritically. Just as librarians believe they have a role in helping children develop critical reading skills, they also have a responsibility to help children develop critical listening and viewing skills. Children need to learn what and what not to believe and to be selective in what they choose to listen to and to view.

One way to help develop critical skills is to provide children the opportunity to experience what is not widely available on radio or television, in the video or record shops, or at movie theaters. Any child whose book exposure is limited to what is found in grocery stores, or even many bookstores, misses many of the best books. The same is true for the child whose only selection of cassettes is what is available at a record store or whose only viewing experience is television or rented videos. By giving children the opportunity to see and listen to quality materials, the library helps children learn to evaluate what they see and hear with open minds and a critical eye.

Criteria for selection of nonprint materials parallel those for books in many ways, but they must take into account the unique properties of each type of material. Nonprint collections must also reflect both quality and popularity. Librarians can find help in selection from reviews and bibliographies. A good example is the lists of films, filmstrips, and recordings published annually by the American Library Association. *Booklist, School Library Journal,* and other library periodicals review nonprint materials, and specialist periodicals which concentrate on one type of material are available.

VIDEOTAPE AND FILM

Film has been widely used in libraries, and public libraries often circulate films to community organizations and individuals. In schools they have been used for classroom instruction. Frequently, film collections, because of cost, are centrally purchased on a state, regional, or district basis and available to libraries through advance booking or on a rotating library circuit. The development of easy, inexpensive videotape technology is causing a revolution in visual technology. Whereas film projectors are expensive, and their availability limited, videotape equipment is available in schools, homes, and elsewhere. For many uses, it is now the preferred format because of ease of use and portability as well as availability of equipment. As equipment for large screen projection becomes more widely available and video quality improves, the use of 16mm film will continue to decrease and may eventually become obsolete. Videotapes are almost always much less expensive than films, making it possible for more libraries to develop their own collections for circulation.

Many videotapes purchased by libraries for circulation to the public are licensed for home use only and cannot be used by the library for a public performance and should not be loaned to anyone planning to use them for a public performance. Public libraries may not rent videotapes from video shops to show at programs since these are also restricted to home use. If a library wants to use

videotapes at programs, it must obtain a public performance license for a substantial fee from the copyright owner. Schools may use home-use videotapes for educational purposes only. Therefore, they can show a feature film licensed for home use if it is connected to instruction, but not if it is entertainment for a class party or non-instructional activity. Many educational and documentary programs are not restricted to home use only, but libraries should be sure before using them for programs.

Schools may copy a television program and keep it for 45 days although they may show it only twice during the first ten school days. Public libraries may not copy television programs to show at a later date. Copying a program and adding it to a library collection violates copyright law (Reed and Stanek, 1986).

Children's films and videotapes cover many subjects and approaches. A collection may include three-minute films where changing shapes and lively music provide experiences in color and sound, cartoon stories, films based on children's books and stories, documentaries, mood and concept films, and films just for fun. Many children have access to films at home through cable television or home video. However, the average video store collection emphasizes very popular film titles, cartoons, and television programs popular with children. They often do not provide children with the opportunity to see a wide variety of high-quality productions. A carefully developed library collection offers children and their families the opportunity to experience films they would otherwise miss.

In selecting films or videotapes, it is important to evaluate both technical quality and content as well as appeal for children. Films that introduce children to new experiences, other cultures, ideas, and feelings will help them stretch their minds and inspire and educate, as well as entertain.

Evaluating technical quality requires examination of the techniques used in making the film such as photography, animation, sound, editing, and acting. Photography should be sharp and clear with good color. It should be effective and imaginative in its use of visual images and in its composition so that it is interesting to view. Animation should be smooth and convincing. In mediocre animation, movement may be very limited, choppy and unnatural looking. Puppet animation, in particular, is sometimes very stiff and awkward if it is not done well. Look for films that use a style of animation which children may not have previously seen such as peanut or clay animation. In live-action films, acting should be believable and well done. Actors should have clear diction and good voice quality. Scenery or sets should suit the style of the film. Sound should be clear and voices easily understood. Any narration should be interesting and not overly pedantic. Many children's animated films are foreign, and any dubbing should be well done. Both music and narration should synchronize well with the visual images. Music should be high quality and should suit the style and theme of the film. The film should move smoothly so viewers are unaware of editing. It is important that the film is an appropriate length, neither so long that it drags or bores viewers nor so short that important information or incidents are unclear.

Evaluating the film for content is determining how well the film accomplishes what it is trying to do. If the film is a documentary, it must be accurate and should present information in a way that is interesting and informative to children. Looking at common things or activities from a child's viewpoint or letting them see behind the scenes will give children new insight. Taking advantage of the film technology may allow them to see animals or places in ways a book cannot equal.

If the film is based on a story or book, it should be faithful to the original. Any added or changed incidents should be in keeping with the spirit of the original and not change its essential theme or impact. For example, a film that adds a strong moral lesson to a folktale or that makes it saccharine or overly cute would be changing the story's intent. The best films may give viewers a new understanding of the implications of the story. Consider also if the story works as a film. Some books translate beautifully into film. Some even are more successful than in the book format. Others lose feeling and impact as films. The fact that the book is good is no guarantee that the story will be successful on film. A film must work as a film as well as retelling the story.

If the film used an original script, the story should be high quality with good characterizations. Narration or dialogue should be appropriate to the film and should not talk down to children. The choice of medium, whether live action or animation, should fit the story or subject. Many films are experimental or experiential in nature, offering children an opportunity to see something in a new and different way or to experience light, color, form, or images around a theme but without a plot. These can be great mind-stretchers, but they need to be accessible to children on at least some level.

Most public libraries want to consider if a film is for circulation or has program potential for use by the library. School media centers need to determine its appropriateness to classroom use. In either case, a film may serve as a lead-in to other activities.

Libraries may select film and video from reviews and by previewing them. Preview privileges are generally available from film distributors to schools and libraries with a budget for purchase and serious intent to buy.

FILMSTRIPS

Filmstrips are a series of still pictures on a continuous piece of film. Most filmstrips come with a cassette tape soundtrack. Generally, filmstrip projectors have a built-in tape player that will synchronize the two and automatically advance the frames of the filmstrip. Where small filmstrip projectors without a player are used, a separate tape player can be used and the frames advanced manually. Many children's books and stories as well as original stories are available on filmstrips. Filmstrips are also available on a variety of subjects.

Filmstrips have been used more widely in schools than in public libraries. They are used for instruction in many classrooms, for introducing books, and for individual viewing. In public libraries they may be circulated to day care centers and other groups, used with an individual projector that allows children to watch them on their own in the library, or used in programs.

One of the appeals of filmstrips to both school and public libraries has been their low cost compared to 16mm films. They are easier to use and to store. However, being made of a series of stills that advance, they can tend to appear stiff, and in general they are less compelling than a moving image. With the growth of videotape, often available at close to the same cost, filmstrip use may decline in the future.

The quality of filmstrips varies widely. They need to be selected from reviews or purchased on approval so that poor or mediocre materials can be rejected. Filmstrips are often marketed in sets or special packages, which can save money, but they may be of inconsistent quality. It is not recommended that librarians select filmstrips from catalogs. Filmstrips that if they were in book format would not meet the standards of the collection should not be purchased.

If filmstrip pictures are taken from book illustrations, they should be accurately reproduced. They should not be overly blown up or poorly cropped just to fit a frame. They should be clear and not grainy. If the filmstrip is based on a book but has new illustrations, the pictures should fit the story and be of a quality comparable to the original book illustrations. Otherwise, in most situations, it would be preferable to use the book with children. If the illustrations were drawn for the filmstrip they should meet the artistic standards of books in the collection. Colors should not be bright and gaudy or overly cartoonish just to attract attention. Characters should be convincingly drawn and not stereotypes. Settings and costumes should be consistent and appropriate to the story or subject.

The soundtrack should be clear and easy to understand. Narration and dialogue should be well written and voices should not be saccharine or overly dramatic. Sound effects and music should be of good quality and suited to the story. If the filmstrip is based on a book it should follow the text. Any added narration or dialogue should fit the mood and rhythm of the original. Filmstrips based on longer books and novels are likely to be shortened. It is preferable to abridge the original text rather than rewrite it. The text should retain the feeling of the book and not focus only on recounting the plot. When the filmstrip is based on a folk or fairy tale, narration should suit the story and setting. Versions with new endings or in which major events are changed to soften the story or add a moral lesson should be avoided. Extraneous characters such as Donald Duck or other cartoon heroes used as story characters or narrators can take attention away from the story or event being told. In original stories, characters should be true to their type and not be prettified for children. For example, a monster should act like a monster, not like a buddy. Avoid stories which are thinly veiled moral lessons. The story should be able to stand on its own as a good quality story.

Nonfiction filmstrips should provide information accurately and clearly with a good quality, interesting narration. Language and length should be appropriate for the intended audience. Illustrations and photographs should be well done and add to the understanding of the topic.

RECORDINGS

Recordings can be a wonderful way of introducing songs, music, poetry, and stories to children. Most public libraries have records or cassette tapes for circulation and for listening in the library. School libraries may make them available for classroom use as well. Whether a library has records or cassettes or both is a matter of choice. With the introduction of compact discs and other new recording technologies, the choice may be widened. Cassettes are now widely used because they do not scratch and warp like records, but they are not trouble free. Tapes can get jammed in machines and break, especially when machine heads are dirty. Some recordings are available in only a single format.

While recordings are most heavily used for circulation and listening, they are also useful in programs. Recordings can be used as incidental music to open and close programs. They are good sources of songs. While it is preferable to sing with children without a recording, recordings can be played while a group sings. Other recordings provide movement exercises and activities that are useful at story hours. There are many recordings of fine storytelling, which the storyteller can use as a source of new stories and techniques. Recordings can also be used as a resource for librarians, teachers, and other adults.

Recordings should be selected from reviews or recommended lists. For example, a committee of the Association for Library Service to Children compiles an annual list of *Notable Children's Recordings.* Other library associations, periodicals, and large libraries produce discographies. Since high-quality recordings for children are often difficult to find at record and tape shops outside of major cities, they will need to be ordered from record distributors or producers. Finding the titles desired and replacing them can be inconvenient and difficult, and many librarians maintain a file of catalogs to assist with this.

Voices should be pleasant to listen to and natural, clear, and easy to understand. Recordings with overdramatized or saccharine voices or which use a condescending tone should be avoided. Abridgement is often necessary because of length limitations, but the recording should retain the flavor of the original and not be watered down. Sound effects should enhance but not overwhelm the story. The collection of spoken word recordings should include retellings of folk and fairy tales, myths, and legends; readings of picture books and stories for older children; poetry; and book-recording packages which include a book and a recording that allows children to listen and follow along in the book.

Music recordings should be of high quality. Singing voices that capture children's interest and invite them to sing along are often more important than outstanding voice quality. The collection should include lullabies, folk and other children's songs, as well as movie, show, and classical music. Classical pieces should be recommended for or written for children.

Rock and other popular music which is suitable for children can be included as well. However, the fine line between censoring and selection must be considered with lyrics that deal explicitly with drugs and sex. Careful selection for a children's collection is a necessity. These recordings also date quickly, requiring more weeding and updating. However, rock and other popular music is very popular with some children and should not be overlooked completely.

A collection should also include creative activity and movement records, sound effects, and documentary recordings which enhance understanding of historical events.

COMPUTER SOFTWARE

With the increasing importance of computers, more and more libraries are making computer use available to patrons. Many school library media centers function as the computer center or repository for software for their schools. Students may use the computers to complete assignments, learn new skills, or access information. Teachers may borrow software to use on classroom computers much as they borrow books and other materials to use in the classroom. In public libraries, computers and software may be purchased for public use.

Some libraries circulate computer software and even small personal computers. Circulation poses a problem of dealing with a variety of computers which use different operating systems and require different versions of software. Whether a library

purchases software for in-library use or for circulation, it is important to select software for children carefully. With the explosion of computer purchases both by schools and by individuals for home use, a tremendous number of programs for children have been written. Thousands of programs are available, but much of what is available is at best mediocre. Perhaps as little as five percent of software is of sufficiently high quality to be enthusiastically recommended.

Computer programs for children can be categorized into several types. Drill and practice programs or computer assisted instruction allow users to practice skills. Answers to questions are limited to simple responses such as yes or no, and feedback is given immediately. This is the most widely available type of software, but it is also the least desirable. Drill and practice programs are analogous to worksheets and provide passive rather than active learning, even though they are made more exciting by creative use of animation, color, and sound. They take little advantage of the computer's possibilities. The skills reinforced on these programs can often be done as effectively off the computer. Drill and practice programs have a place but should be recognized for what they are.

A second type of software is interactive. A greater variety of responses is possible, and users can determine the direction the program takes by their responses. This type of program can adapt itself to users' individual levels of understanding and skills. Because the children are in control, this type of software is more enjoyable to use and encourages children to stretch themselves and take an active role in learning. Some tutorial programs which are used to teach new material fit into this category, as do many games and simulation programs. The latter allow users to simulate experiences such as piloting an airplane or running a town.

A third type is problem-solving software, which encourages children to find their own solutions. This is the highest level of program and requires use of creative thinking skills. Software, for example, that encourages children to explore a computer language and figure out how it works would be problem solving. This type of software offers flexible, creative experiences that let children discover relationships on their own. Children may have more questions and require more assistance with

FIGURE 3. Children use BookBrain℗, a software program which helps them select books.

problem-solving software, but it offers them the opportunity for active learning.

Also in the area of creative learning is software which is a tool to allow children to create something totally their own on a blank screen. Word processing, graphics, and drawing software are good examples of this. Children like writing on the computer and often produce longer and more creative stories because the ease of correction, the ability to edit and change, and the freedom from recopying remove much of the drudgery from writing.

In selecting software, look for a variety of types for a variety of ages and abilities. Choose programs that will hold children's interest for more than one use. Be sure any software purchased will run on the library computer or on computers for which the library purchases software. Limit purchases of drill software to the best of what is available. Avoid drill programs which express displeasure at wrong responses by devices such as an unhappy face or unpleasant sound because these give children a sense of failure. Be sure content is accurate, without spelling and grammatical errors.

The program should be easy to use with clear instructions and documentation and tools such as help screens and menus. This is especially important for library use where assistance may be limited. At the same time, include programs for the children who are knowledgeable about computers and have the skill and enthusiasm to figure out how to use more challenging programs. Good animation is desirable, but it should be used in a way that aids rather than distracts from using the program fully. Some programs give such a dramatic response for incorrect answers, they encourage children to answer wrong so they can enjoy the animation. Sound levels of music or voices should be adjustable to reduce distraction of others. Libraries will probably want to avoid programs with excessive violence. School media centers will want to consider a program's relationship to curriculum objectives and its usefulness in the classroom as well. Public libraries will want to balance fun and entertainment software with software that can help children learn and even do school assignments.

It may be possible to purchase some software locally where there is an opportunity to try it out. Other programs may be available on approval. Fortunately, there is a wide variety of sources for evaluations of computer software, including such standard library periodicals as *School Library Journal* and *Booklist*.

TOYS AND OTHER REALIA

Another type of material increasingly included in library collections is realia. These include toys, games, puppets, and other hands-on materials. Some libraries have developed circulating toy collections, especially for younger children. Others have limited their realia to specific types such as puppets or puzzles. School media centers often include toys or games that can reinforce newly learned skills or information.

Toys and other hands-on materials are important learning materials. Play is the way young children learn, and hands-on experience with a variety of toys can help them master the skills they need to learn to read successfully. Good toys can aid in the development of the whole child. They help children learn cognitive or learning skills. Playing with others teaches social skills. They develop physically through toys that require use of small and large motor skills. They grow emotionally as success in mastering toys builds self confidence and self concept.

While most people would agree toys are important for children, they may question why libraries should have them. Surely parents can buy toys for their children. However, the same argument could be made about books. Good toys, like good books, are expensive. Many are used only for a short time before children grow beyond them. A library can offer a greater variety of toys to children than most families can afford. It can also allow parents to try toys with their children before purchasing them. By working with parents and providing information on ways a toy can be used, the library can help parents see the importance of play and the value of quality toys. Toys can also be useful to child care programs, which can borrow a toy to work on a special skill, and especially to family day-care homes, where a wide variety of toys may not be available.

In planning a realia collection, it is important to consider carefully your purposes and to choose materials which fit those purposes. It is also important to examine the inherent difficulties with some toys, such as missing pieces, awkward handling and storage, and necessary cleaning and maintenance, and to be prepared to deal with these. Puzzles and toys with essential parts missing should be replaced or repaired, not circulated. Ordering several of the same toy allows one to be used for replacement parts and helps meet the demand on very popular items. Many of the easily available toys are of poor quality. Many of the more creative toys are available only through specialized shops or special orders.

In selecting appropriate toys for the collection, there are several things to consider. First, the toy should be a good toy. This means it should do what it sets out to do well and in a way that the child for whom it is intended can play with it successfully. Good toys encourage creative play; look for ones which are versatile and can be used in more than one way. Choose toys designed to help children learn and develop and not those only for entertainment. Be sure the toy is safe without sharp edges and small parts, particularly if it is for children under age three. For library use, it must be well made and sturdy. Toys also must be practical to circulate. Very large and heavy items, or toys with many pieces, all of which must be there to use are examples of toys difficult to circulate. The most basic of toys—trucks, blocks, and dolls—are ones which a child needs to have available all the time and not for a short circulation. The same is true of stuffed animals, to which children can get very attached.

Don't limit the selection to toys, per se. Include items such as magnifying glasses and prisms that children can use to explore, puppets and costumes for dramatic play, and rhythm and other simple instruments. All toys do not have to be purchased. In fact, including some homemade toys can help parents realize they can make toys for their own children. Feely bags, texture boards, sound cans, and puppets are examples of simple toys that could be made by volunteers.

To make a toy collection effective, it should be combined with workshops for parents on how to use toys with children. Children's area staff should be trained in children's play and how to recommend toys.

BIBLIOGRAPHY

Billinsky, Christyn. "Children's Software: Designs for Learning." *Top of the News* 39 (Summer 1983): 315-320.

Carter, Yvonne B. and Barbara Spreistersbach. *Aids to Media Selection for Students and Teachers.* McFarland, WI: National Association of State Educational Media, 1985.

Children's and Young Adults Services Section. Recordings for Children Committee. *Recordings for Children; A Selected List of Records and Cassettes.* New York: New York Library Association, 1980.

Connecticut Realia Committee. *Toys to Go; A Guide to the Use of Realia in Public Libraries.* Chicago: American Library Association, 1975.

Ellison, John W. and Patricia Ann Coty, eds. *Nonbook Media: Collection Management and User Services.* Chicago: American Library Association, 1987.

Gaffney, Maureen. *More Films Kids Like.* Chicago: American Library Association, 1977.

Giacoma, P. "Computers, Literacy, and Access in the Children's Room." *Top of the News* 41 (Fall 1984): 53-59.

Goldstein, Ruth M. and Edith Zornow. *Movies for Kids; A Guide for Parents and Teachers on the Entertainment Film for Children.* Rev. ed. New York: Frederick Ungar, 1980.

Hammond, Ray. *Computers and Your Child.* New York: Ticknor and Fields, 1984.

Hunt, Mary Alice, ed. *A Multimedia Approach to Children's Literature.* 3rd ed. Chicago: American Library Association, 1983.

Lathrop, Ann. "Microcomputer Courseware: Selection and Evaluation." *Top of the News* 39 (Spring 1983): 265-272.

"Microcomputers and Library Services to Children and Young Adults." Parts 1, 2. *Top of the News* 39 (Spring and Summer 1984): 237-281, 307-351.
> Numerous articles on selection and use in a two-issue feature.

Oppenheim, Joanne F. *Buy Me! Buy Me!: The Bank Street Guide to Choosing Toys for Children.* New York: Pantheon, 1987.

Pagnoni, Mario. *Computers and Small Fries: A Computer-Readiness Guide for Parents of Tots, Toddlers, and Other Minors.* Wayne, NJ: Avery Publishing Group, 1987.
> Includes good list of suggested software for young children.

Reed, Mary Hutchings and Debra Stanek. "Library and Classroom Use of Copyrighted Videotapes and Computer Software." *American Libraries* 17 (Feb 1986): A-D (Insert).

Rice, Susan. *Films Kids Like.* Chicago: American Library Association, 1971.

Sinker, Mary. *Toys for Growing: A Guide to Toys That Develop Skills.* Published for the National Lekotek Center. Chicago: Year Book Medical Publishers, 1986.

The Video Source Book. Syosset, NY: National Video Clearinghouse. Annual.

Woolls, Blanche. "Selecting Microcomputer Software for the Library." *Top of the News* 39 (Summmer 1983): 321-327.

Collection Maintenance and Reevaluation

Collection reevaluation, most commonly known as weeding, is the process of removing books and other materials from the library collection when they are no longer useful. It is an essential part of collection development. A good weeding policy and procedure is as important as good selection procedures in building and maintaining an attractive and useful collection.

Because it is a task many librarians don't enjoy, weeding is often put off until space is needed. However, overcrowded shelves should not be the first or only motivation for weeding. Instead, it should be motivated by a desire to maintain an up-to-date, inviting, and useful collection. Just as weeds can overtake a garden and hide the beauty of flowers, materials left in the library collection which are no longer useful can make it more difficult to find the ones which are.

Withdrawal of books and other materials should be done on the basis of condition, usefulness, and use by patrons. Books and other materials in poor physical condition should be withdrawn. Worn-out, soiled, or damaged books with missing pages, tears, grease or food stains, and crayon or other coloring are good candidates for withdrawal. Leaving books with coloring, food stains, or dirt on the shelves leads children to believe that coloring in books or dropping food in them is acceptable. It is important for libraries to give the impression that books—including library books—are special and desirable. Dirty books are not appealing. In the same way, records that are badly scratched, films with many scratch lines, and puzzles with missing pieces are no longer useful for the collection.

Materials which are dated should also be withdrawn. It is especially important with children to keep nonfiction collections up-to-date because they often will not have the background to recognize when information is dated. As information and technology change, information in books and nonprint materials may become inaccurate, making the materials obsolete. For example, books on subjects such as computers or space flight date rapidly. Older materials may be accurate but not include information about recent developments and events, and the lack of new information makes them misleading. Materials which were published about countries before major changes in governments are good examples of this. Views or interpretations of a subject may have changed, making the slant or approach dated. A good example here is books on foreign countries which focus on quaint aspects of their culture rather then showing how people live today. Illustrations, photographs, or format can also date materials.

Fiction and picture books can also become dated. Children may be dressed in dated clothing, sexual and racial roles may be stereotyped, and the story may not have appeal for children today, just to give a few examples. The best books have illustrations and text which have continuing appeal even though some parts of them may appear old-fashioned.

Even award-winning books should be reevaluated. While larger libraries will want to have a complete set of Newbery and Caldecott Medal books, smaller libraries may not be able to justify shelf space for those titles which no longer attract readers. Even when children are assigned award books to read, certain titles may never circulate. Of all book awards for children, the Newbery and Caldecott Awards have taken on a special aura. Most libraries would not be expected to have all Pulitzer books from the 1930s, for example, and yet the Newbery and Caldecott Medal books are often considered sacred. Certainly a library should have a good selection of these titles, but winning the award should not necessarily mean immortality for all the books.

Books which are no longer used or have never been used should be considered for withdrawal. All book selectors make mistakes, and most libraries contain books that have sat on the shelf for years and look brand new because they never have been used. It is important to try to determine why a book was not be used. It may have been classified in a strange number. It may have an unusual title or unattractive cover. If a book is still worthwhile, try to interest children in the book by displaying it and putting it on booklists before discarding it.

Finally, overcrowding is a consideration in weeding. Book shelves are most inviting when they are not overcrowded. Ideally, there should be room at the end of shelves to display books face out. Overcrowded shelves discourage browsing. Patrons do not like having to force a book on or off tightly packed shelves.

Bibliographies and booklists can be helpful tools in weeding. No librarian can know the quality of every book in the collection, and most librarians have subject areas about which they know little. Checking to see if books are in standard bibliographies can help in the decision of whether to withdraw, replace, or leave in the collection. Checking bibliographies, however, is time consuming, and it is important to remember that they are subjective. They also don't help evaluate the collection in relation to your community or school curriculum. Just because a book in the collection is not listed does not mean it isn't adequate for the collection.

Also helpful are weeding guidelines which suggest number of years since publication before books in any one subject become dated. These are guidelines, however, not rules. While a book on a rapidly changing Third World country may date quickly, a book on a more settled country in Western Europe may be useful for a longer period. Local subject experts such as teachers can be helpful in determining whether information is dated.

It is also important to know your community and users and how the collection is currently used before weeding. New librarians should allow time to get to know the collection and the patrons before weeding extensively. Weeding in the first year on the job should be limited to only the most obvious items, such as books which say we will reach the moon someday or those which are falling apart. Waiting can be difficult, but when librarians know the collection and the users better, and the staff know the children's librarian, weeding will be less threatening to everyone. Spend time learning the collection and identifying areas needing the most immediate attention. Begin to order new titles in areas that will need to be heavily weeded.

Statistics about the collection and its use can also be helpful. A computerized circulation system identifies which books have not circulated in a specified period or which areas of the collection are most heavily used. This can be useful in establishing priority areas of the collection for reevaluation. However, circulation information is only one factor. The book may be a basic title in an area where requests are infrequent but may be worth retaining.

Whatever resources are used, they do not replace the importance of critical judgment on the part of librarians. On the first weeding of a collection it is preferable to retain some questionable titles rather than to discard books that are later missed.

Routine weeding should be done on a continuous basis as librarians see books that are obviously worn out or outdated. However, every library also needs to evaluate regularly each area of the collection in a logical and systematic way. It can be overwhelming to try to examine an entire collection as one big project. A schedule for weeding should be designed so that the entire collection is examined every three to five years. An example of a five-year weeding schedule would be:

Year 1	000-399	Fiction A-G
Year 2	400-599	Fiction H-P
Year 3	600-799	Fiction Q-Z
Year 4	800-999	Picture Books A-K
Year 5	Biographies	Picture Books L-Z

In addition to making the task manageable, using a schedule such as this will allow for regular replacement and updating and avoid the need for massive replacement orders in any one year.

Books withdrawn from the collection because of condition should be considered for replacement. Titles which should be replaced include popular titles and titles listed in standard bibliographies which the librarian believes should be in the collection. A shabby appearance alone can discourage browsers; ordering a new, attractive copy of a standard title can often change it from a shelf sitter to a book which is read. Worn nonfiction in many cases will be replaced by newer titles. It is important to keep track of subjects where new books are needed.

A weeding of the fiction collection may mean that many books in one genre need to be replaced. Rather than reordering many older mystery or sports titles, librarians may prefer to replace only the best and to try to order more heavily from newer titles being published. Because of the frequency with which books go out of print, replacement of all desired titles may not be possible. A book may be available only in paperback or not at all. If pages are in good condition, rebinding is a possibility. However, with children's books this should be a last resort because the plain bindings tend to discourage children from selecting them.

Each library needs to have a written procedure for withdrawal and disposal of materials. Generally, the librarian removes any books which need discarding or replacing. Some of the books which need replacing may need to be left on the shelves until new copies can be received especially if the budget does not allow immediate replacement. Old copies should then be removed when replacements arrive. Discarding books, including removing ownership marks and clearing records, should be done according to the library's set procedure. The shelf list is marked and catalog cards or computer entry removed if needed.

The method of disposal is determined by library or school policy. Many libraries destroy withdrawn books although some choose to sell them at book sales. Destroying them eliminates their com-

ing back to the library. Also, old, dated, and worn material, no longer suited to the library collection, is usually of little use to anyone else. It is not a good idea to give discarded books to schools, child care centers, children's homes, and other needy groups because worn, dated books will not meet the needs of the children and will in fact give the recipients the idea that library books are like those being given. It is preferable to offer library service instead.

School media centers may have less freedom than public libraries because of the need to meet numerical requirements for numbers of volumes for school accreditation. If the collection is in poor condition, it may be necessary to convince the administration of the need for special funds for replacement before undertaking a large-scale weeding project. Good documentation showing the average age of books in particular subject areas can provide a convincing argument. Sometimes, parent-teacher organizations will raise special funds for this type of project.

Nonprint materials need to be weeded as well. Records become scratched and warped, and popular music, especially, may become dated. Filmstrips, films, and videotapes may be scratched and can become faded over time. Documentary and other factual material may become dated both in the text and visuals. Parts of toys may be missing or broken. While much of this may show up through routine checking, it is necessary to examine the entire collection systematically from time to time.

BIBLIOGRAPHY

Buckingham, Betty Jo. *Weeding the Library Media Center Collections.* Des Moines, IA: State of Iowa Department of Public Instruction, 1984.

Segal, Joseph P. *Evaluating and Weeding Collections in Small and Medium-Sized Public Libraries: The CREW Method.* Chicago: American Library Association, 1980.

Slote, Stanley. *Weeding Library Collections-II.* Littleton, CO: Libraries Unlimited, 1982.

Censorship is a way of making something unavailable because of objections to its contents. Books, films, and recordings have been censored by governments, religious and other organizations, and by the efforts of individuals. Censors may want to suppress certain ideas and viewpoints or to keep others from reading, hearing, or viewing something they find objectionable. Someone once asked which one of your neighbors would you want to decide what you and your family could read as a way of pinpointing the difficulties and potential dangers involved in limiting what people read.

While the Bill of Rights has traditionally provided a strong defense against censorship in the United States, attempts to censor items in library collections occur with regularity. Libraries have usually tried to stand up for intellectual freedom, the right of individuals to read or view whatever they choose. The American Library Association has a special Office of Intellectual Freedom and an Intellectual Freedom Committee. State library associations generally also have intellectual freedom committees. There is also a National Coalition Against Censorship.

Attempts to have books removed from libraries are frequently directed at children's and young adult books. While we often think of censorship attempts as coming only from those who are very conservative, this is not true. People who request that books be removed because of sexism, ageism, pro-hunting views, or whatever, are also trying to keep people from reading about things they consider wrong. Librarians can also be censors by avoiding purchase of anything they feel might be controversial in an attempt to avoid challenges by patrons. Allowing personal beliefs and viewpoints

to determine book selection can also be a form of censorship. The librarian who refuses to buy books about warplanes because she believes they encourage war is censoring. While librarians must be sensitive to communities in developing collections, it is safe to say that no community, even one that is small and isolated, is completely homogeneous. To allow prevailing viewpoints to determine all selection is to limit those who may think differently.

Censorship requests take all forms. Some may be understandable, others incomprehensible. Parents may object to bad language or specific incidents. They may object to a theme which goes against their convictions. Some people object to children reading books about magic; others object to things that are not true, such as fantasy, or things which are violent. Objections can run to the absurd. One library had a patron complain about *Ellen Tebbits* by Beverly Cleary because the heroine wears a short tutu on the cover! Many complaints center on sex education or sexual incidents. Whatever the complaint, it is important to treat patrons with respect. While librarians are unlikely to change parents' viewpoints, they may be able to help them realize that other parents see issues differently and that the library exists to serve everyone.

The "Free Access to Libraries for Minors" statement adopted by the American Library Association Council in 1972 and amended in 1981 states that:

> The American Library Association opposes libraries restricting access to library materials and services for minors and holds that it is the parents—and only parents—who may restrict their children—and only their children—from access to library materials and services. Parents who would rather their children did not have

access to certain materials should so advise their children. The library and its staff are responsible for providing equal access to library materials and services for all library users.

This statement says that while parents may choose to restrict their own children's reading, they do not have the right to impose these restrictions on other children in the community whose parents may wish their children to have greater freedom in selecting materials or who choose to limit in a different way.

School libraries are probably subject to more complaints about materials than public libraries, partly because parents tend to keep a closer eye on what children are doing at school. Concern about negative publicity having an impact on a school district can cause considerable pressure to be put on librarians to simply remove a book that is questioned. Public librarians are certainly not immune to similar pressures, and most librarians encounter questions about materials in the collection at least occasionally.

The best approach is to be well prepared. All libraries should have written policies and procedures for selection which can be discussed with patrons. Libraries should also have a standard procedure for addressing citizen complaints. Many libraries use a form which they request be filled out by the person making the complaint. The questions should not be written in a patronizing way, which could further upset the complainant. (See sample form in this chapter.)

The library should have a procedure so that the request can be channeled through the proper chain of command. Circulation staff should refer questions to the staff member in charge of the department concerned. Questions about children's materials should be referred to the children's department. All librarians should be familiar with the Library Bill of Rights and other statements on intellectual freedom. Librarians working with children should also make special efforts to read books and view and listen to other materials which you suspect might be controversial. By making organizations such as library Friends groups and parent teacher organizations aware of the library's philosophy about the freedom to read, libraries can build a base of support if it is ever needed.

Treat patrons who question materials with respect. They have a right to be concerned and probably would not have bothered to question the library unless they felt strongly about the item. Hos-tility or defensiveness by library staff will only make people more determined. Begin by trying to discuss their concerns informally. Often, librarians' willingness to listen to and talk with patrons about their concerns can defuse the issue. Explain the library's selection policy and procedure. Admit if you have not read the book, and inform the patron that staff will need to do so before responding to specific concerns. As much as possible, however, focus on the principles of intellectual freedom rather than the specific item in question. If the patron wants to file a formal complaint, explain the procedure and provide the form, assuring the patron that the objections will be considered.

SAMPLE: Citizen's Request for Reconsideration of Library Material

To the person requesting reconsideration:

Library policy requires that complaints be filed on this form. A copy of the library's materials selection policy will be made available to you. Thank you for taking the time to provide this information.

Author_____

Title_____

Publisher or producer_____

Request initiated by_____

Telephone_____

Address_____

City_____

Zip code_____

Do you represent:

Yourself:_____

Name of organization:_____

Name of other group:_____

1. Specifically, what are your objections? (Cite pages, instances, etc.)_____
2. What do you believe might be the result of reading, hearing, or seeing this material?_____
3. Is there anything good about this material?____
4. Did you read the entire book or examine the entire item?_____
5. What do you believe is the theme of this material?_____
6. What would you like to have the library do about this material?
   _____Do not lend it to my child.
   _____Return it to the staff selection committee or department for reevaluation.

Other_____

Date:_____

Signature:_____

When a complaint is filed, try to locate reviews or listings in bibliographies. The patron may not care what experts say, but reviews will help show why the item was purchased. If the circulation system makes it possible, note how many times the book has circulated or how many years it has been in the library without complaints being made about it. Reread or reexamine the item, and ask one or more other staff members to do so as well. Try to understand the patron's viewpoint about the book, and be open to the possibility the library may have made a poor selection. Be prepared to defend a book or other item that staff feels is worthwhile. Keep supervisors informed about complaints and prepare a report with your recommendations and a draft response. It is important that administrators know about complaints, so they will not be caught by surprise if they are asked about it or if the patron seeks publicity in the effort to remove the item.

Moving items to restricted locations, putting them in adult collections, or requiring parental permission to use items are really ways of avoiding the issue. They effectively remove the book from children but allow the library to say it did not remove the item. If material for children is worth having, it should be on the open shelves and accessible to children.

Following a clear procedure and treating complaints with respect will defuse most situations. In recent years, however, there have been organized groups coming to libraries with lists of books they want removed. Occasionally, a patron insists on going directly to the library or school board or to governmental officials and seeks media attention. When a censorship attempt reaches the press, it raises community emotions and puts the library in a more difficult position as well as ensuring that many children will rush to read or see the item in question. The library staff should try to defuse the situation by remaining calm and logical and keeping focused on the issue of the freedom to read rather than on the item being questioned. The library must rely on its good public relations and reputation and other citizens' concerns about the long-range implications of removing books and other materials. Unfortunately, in situations where material removal requests become public issues, the library cannot win. Even when the issue is resolved in the library's favor, it has negative public relations effects. Try to avoid problems by dealing openly with questions as they arise and working to avoid their becoming a larger issue.

BIBLIOGRAPHY

American Library Association. Office of Intellectual Freedom. *Intellectual Freedom Manual.* Chicago: American Library Association, 1983.

Association for Library Service to Children. *Intellectual Freedom for Children: A Packet of Materials.* Rev. ed. Chicago: American Library Association, 1986.

Donalson, Ken. "Censorship." *Prelude, Series #6.* New York: Children's Book Council, 1981 (cassette).

"Free Access to Library Service for Minors: An Interpretation of the Library Bill of Rights. Amended 1981." *Top of the News* 38 (Fall 1981): 12-13.

Jones, Frances M. *Defusing Censorship: The Librarian's Guide to Handling Censorship Conflicts.* Phoenix, AZ: Oryx Press, 1983.

Morrill, Richard L. "School Library Media Programs and Intellectual Freedom; An Examination of Major Court Cases." *School Library Media Quarterly* 14 (Winter 1986): 71-82.

Oboler, Eli. *Defending Intellectual Freedom; The Library and the Censor.* Westwood, CT: Greenwood Press, 1980.

Oboler, Eli, ed. *Censorship and Education.* Westwood, CT: Greenwood Press, 1981.

Reichman, Henry. *Censorship and Selection: Issues and Answers for Schools.* Chicago: American Library Association, 1988.

Robotham, John and Gerald Shields. *Freedom of Access to Library Materials.* New York: Neal-Schuman, 1982.

Helping Children Use the Collection

Reference and reader's advisory services are the major responsibilities of librarians working with children. Children's librarians need the same skills as reference librarians but have a different body of literature as the basic collection. Unless children receive the help needed in using the collection, its use is greatly limited. Children ask lots of questions, and many are every bit as challenging as those posed by adults. It is important that staff knowledgeable about the collection and skilled in dealing with children be available to help.

Knowledge of the collection is acquired gradually and should grow as long as librarians are working. Children's literature courses can offer librarians only a tip of the iceberg. All librarians working with children need to continually extend and deepen their knowledge of children's books and other materials by becoming familiar with and reading both new and older materials. It is also their responsibility to try and interest other staff in learning more about the collection. It may be possible to give adequate reference service by using the catalog and reference books, but it is impossible to do good reader's advisory work without knowledge of the collection. Librarians working with children should examine all the new children's books and read as many new titles as possible. At the very least, they should read a couple of chapters of new books to get a sense of their flavor and quality. Fiction is perhaps the most difficult area of the collection to really know, but it is essential if librarians are to suggest books effectively and encourage use of books which are not immediately popular.

Librarians should read a variety of types of books, even those of the genres they don't particularly enjoy. They should also be sure to read anything that might be controversial. While it may be enjoyable, it is not as important to read the new "Ramona" or "Paddington" story as it is to read books by unfamiliar or new authors or books that look as if they will need to be sold to children. Encourage staff to share their knowledge of children's books with each other.

It is equally important to become knowledgeable about the nonprint collection. Preview films and filmstrips and become familiar with recordings, computer programs and other materials.

Children, like many adults, often do not know what to ask or what they can expect the library to provide. They may not realize that asking for help is encouraged or that the library can help identify a rock or find a picture of the insides of a vacuum cleaner. Part of providing good services is making people aware of what the library can do.

Children must be made to feel welcome and important in the library. They should not feel less significant than adult users or that their requests are not taken seriously. They should be welcomed and asked if they would like assistance, particularly if they seem to be looking for something specific and are not finding it. Frequently, children will refuse an offer of assistance, not wanting to bother staff. "May I help you?" may elicit a "No," whereas a more open-ended question may get a positive response. "Let me know if there is something I can help you with," "Are you finding what you're looking for?" or "Are you looking for something special today?" These may encourage children to ask for help or make them feel comfortable about coming back for help if they cannot find what they want.

Public librarians should try to offer assistance to everyone entering the area, and avoid answering questions by pointing or telling children to check the card catalog or look on the shelf. Children often need help getting started and understanding how to use tools and find material. If several children need help, it is often necessary to get each one started and then check back as time allows. In the public library, the philosophy is that librarians should help people find information. Going to the shelves and helping them select appropriate materials by pointing out features of different materials on a topic helps to ensure children find what they want. At the same time, librarians should encourage children's efforts to become skilled in using the library independently. In school libraries, where teaching library skills is a central function, more emphasis is placed on encouraging children to find material themselves. Also, in school library media centers children often come in classes or groups, and individual assistance for each child is not practical. Still, library media specialists should be sure children feel comfortable asking for help when it is needed. Whatever the situation, the goal is that children should not leave frustrated and without the material they wanted.

Children's questions generally fall into one of several types. They may ask questions because of personal interest and a sincere desire to know more about the subject. They may ask librarians to suggest a good book to read. Other questions relate to school assignments or club projects. During the school year, assignment-related questions may be the most frequent. Often, children are unsure of what they need, uninterested in the topic, or unclear about how to approach it. They may also come after all the material on a subject has been checked out. Every question children ask is important. Children should not be discriminated against in public libraries because the information requested is for school assignments. Children should also have the same right as adult patrons to request information by telephone without being asked why they want the information. Many public libraries refuse to answer assignment questions by telephone, believing children should find the information themselves. This fails to recognize the fact that many children may not have a way to get to the library. With the increasing availability of informa-

tion data bases, libraries should be sure that their policies do not deny access to children.

Ideally, helping children with assignment-related questions can be made easier if librarians, whether in a school or public library, have good relationships with teachers. School library media specialists may find this easier than public librarians because they work with teachers every day, but they also get caught by unexpected and unclear assignments, and unrealistic demands on a limited amount of resources on a topic. By working together through a joint committee or informally, librarians can help teachers see assignments from the library's viewpoint and encourage teachers to keep the library informed about research assignments. They can present a program at a faculty meeting or in-service day and prepare a brochure about what each library can and cannot do and how they can help. Working together with other librarians can be especially effective. One joint committee eventually convinced a large school district to ban mass assignments, where every child writes on the same subject, and to ban assignments requiring pictures from books or magazines, which encourages mutilation of library materials.

There are also useful strategies for individual librarians. When students come in with a written assignment, copy it, noting the teacher's name and date. This may help when other students from the class come. If students come with reading lists, make a copy. If the list has many books unavailable in your collection, send a note to the teacher. Have a form to give to students to take to their teachers when material is unavailable. This will relieve students' anxiety because teachers will know students tried to find the information, and it may help teachers to realize that sufficient materials may not always be available. (There is a sample form at the end of the chapter.) The goal of teachers and librarians alike should be to have assignments be a positive learning experience. If students find material unavailable, they will develop negative attitudes about reports and about libraries.

Librarians can conduct reference interviews to help understand what children want and need and often to help children clarify for themselves what they want. Librarians first want to know what is the exact information desired. Children may ask for general information when what they want is very specific. For example, a child may ask for books on vegetables when an assignment is to list the vitamins in green beans. Librarians need to ask if the child wants to know about a particular vegetable or whether he or she is interested in growing, cooking, or the biology of vegetables. In many cases children don't know exactly what they want. They may have an assignment to read a biography or to write a science report. The librarian can help find a person they would be interested in reading about or in defining some topic in science that interests them.

Librarians also need to know how much information is needed, how long a report is planned, and if students are to use a specified number of sources. If a child needs to write a one-page biography of George Washington, a reference article or chapter in a book would be more appropriate as a source than a full-length biography. Children may need something they can check out, or they may be restricted from using certain types of sources. Teachers often forbid using encyclopedias or tell students books must be of a certain length. While librarians may not see these restrictions as very useful, the children are expected to follow them. It is also important to determine children's reading levels. Rather than asking, show them books and ask if they can read them or if they have enough detail for their needs.

Once librarians have a clear concept of what the children want, they are ready to help them find it. By explaining each step in the process and involving them in the search, librarians help children learn how to find information themselves. Every question need not be turned into a library skills lesson. On the other hand, librarians want to avoid doing the assignments for children. Sometimes this is a thin line, requiring judgment.

Librarians should encourage children to go beyond the encyclopedia. Useful as they are, encyclopedias are often regarded by children as the easy answer to anything rather than as a starting point. They can be encouraged to use it, when appropriate, and to use other resources as well.

Sometimes all the needed information can't be found in the children's area or library media center. When library media specialists refer children to the public library, or children's librarians refer children to adult reference services, they should send a note explaining what they have already done, so the next person doesn't have to start from scratch. Policies which allow interlibrary loan among all libraries in the service area should be encouraged. With the increased use of computerized networking and information technology, libraries find it easier than ever to access information or locate materials in other locations and arrange to borrow them. Networks are opening up collections of many public and school libraries, and children's books which were sometimes difficult to obtain should become more accessible. Children should not be restricted from interlibrary loan use because of age. However, borrowing libraries must abide by loan policies of some academic and other libraries, which may restrict use by age.

SAMPLE: Parent/Teacher Notification Form

Library _____ Date_____
Dear Parent and/or Teacher:
_____ came to the library today.
We were unable to fill the request for_____
_____
because:

1. _____ All material on the subject is in use.

2. _____ A reasonable search failed to locate suitable material.

3. _____ There are too many restrictions on the types of materials students may use.

4. _____ All material on the subject must be used in the library.

5. _____ Further clarification of the question or topic is needed.

6. _____ We are unable to provide so much on one subject to so many students at one time.

7. _____ Material on this subject is in heavy demand by other people not in this class.

8. _____ The assignment deadline does not allow time for interlibrary loan of materials.

9. _____ Other _____

May we ask that you give us advance notice of assignments so that we may better serve the students? We would welcome a call or visit from you.

Librarian_____
Telephone_____

Reader's advisory questions require different approaches. Children may have specific requests or just want something good to read. Taking time to talk with children about specific books they have enjoyed may help. Parents often request books by reading level. In reader's advisory work, librarians draw heavily on their book knowledge. If the library cannot have trained and knowledgeable personnel available at all times, it is the responsibility of the

FIGURE 4. Children enjoy being able to use the library independently.

librarian in charge to help other staff give good service by sharing information about children's books and making bibliographies available to help identify good books by subject or type. Bibliographies can be very helpful. Both *Children's Catalog* and *Elementary School Library Collection* index fiction by subject. Other bibliographies are arranged by subject or focus on particular subjects or types of books. Preparing booklists on various topics is another form of reader's advisory work, giving children suggestions of books and other materials they may enjoy.

Children's areas and media centers also get requests from adults. Parents and teachers may want books for reading aloud, tapes for a car trip, or information to share with children. People taking children's literature classes make heavy use of library collections. Some adults may want a children's book for an easily understood explanation of a subject, for illustrations, or for information unavailable elsewhere.

Helping people of whatever age use the children's collection is essential to good library service. By providing materials, answers, and information, librarians help them to become comfortable using the library and to learn that the library can be a valuable resource throughout their lives.

BIBLIOGRAPHY

Note: For subject bibliographies helpful in reference and readers' advisory work, see Bibliography in Chapter 4.

Katz, Bill and Ruth A. Fraley, eds. *Reference Services for Children.* New York: Haworth Press, 1983.

Kids Are Patrons Too! Chicago: American Library Association Video, 1987 (videotape).
    Uses examples of librarians doing reference and reader's advisory work with children to show good technique.

Poulette, Nancy. *Books and Real Life: A Guide for Gifted Students and Teachers.* Jefferson, NC: McFarland, 1984.

Zlotnick, Barbara Bradley. *Ready for Reference: Media Skills for Intermediate Students.* Edited by Paula Kay Montgomery. Littleton, CO: Libraries Unlimited, 1984.

For some children's librarians, programming is the most enjoyable part of the job; for others, it is a burden. Programming is probably one reason why children's librarians—especially public librarians who do programs in numerous branches, child care centers, and other facilities on a regular basis—burn out.

Programming may include a variety of activities, from toddler and preschool story programs to family film programs and festivals. Programs and other special activities provide a way to introduce books and the library to children, to offer them new experiences with literature, and to give them enriching educational and cultural experiences. Quality programming can help them understand themselves and others better, provide an alternative to television, and offer them a fun, enjoyable experience. Programming can help make the library's collection come alive for children, and it stimulates use of library materials. It can also provide opportunities to highlight underutilized parts of the collection. Programs also increase the library's visibility in the community or school. For public libraries, programming is also a way to attract new patrons, including those who read little or not at all. Parents who might never come on their own will bring children to programs and may become users themselves.

Library programs may be done in libraries or at other locations in the community where children are—child development centers and recreational and community centers, for example. Library programs may also be done on television where they have the potential to reach far greater numbers. Cable television has opened up many opportunities in this area. Libraries are doing everything from preschool story hours recorded for television to elaborate programming designed especially for the television market.

All library programs should aim to provide a positive library experience for children and to encourage them to use library materials. Library programs should not be done only to increase circulation or to bring in new users, although these are desirable outcomes.

Certain skills are required to do quality programs for children. Librarians must have planning and organizational skills. They must be flexible enough to change plans on short notice and adapt when things don't happen as planned. They must be able keep groups of children under control without stifling them. They must also be creative and able to develop interesting ideas for programs, often on a shoestring budget. Creativity does not mean having to design something totally new, but being able to take an idea and make it work in a particular library or other setting.

When librarians read about good programs or activities, they should write down the ideas and keep them in a file. The time saved by adapting or duplicating a good idea rather than always starting from scratch can better be spent elsewhere. Schools, scout troops, and other organizations, as well as other libraries can be good sources of ideas. Many good ideas come from newspaper coverage of community events, library periodicals, newsletters, and children's books and magazines. Workshops and other training opportunities can provide ideas for programs. It is important to always write for permission before copying any written material and to give credit for ideas when necessary. Librarians in a public library system or school district with numerous librarians are able to share ideas or get assistance from a supervisor or consultant.

It is not necessary for librarians working with children to be masters of all kinds of programs. Some people are spellbinding storytellers and others never more than adequate. Some enjoy using crafts with children, while others find crafts more of a problem than they are worth. Smart librarians draw on their strengths in programming. They utilize other staff skills, ask for volunteer help for other activities, and provide occasional special events by outside groups. Certainly, librarians working with children need to be able to do programs, but sometimes too much stress is put on these skills. Knowledge of materials, interest in collection development, and ability to work with people are equally important.

Volunteers are a wonderful resource. In every community there are potential volunteers. While it may be difficult to find a regular volunteer, people are often willing to help at a special program. A local rock hound, veterinarian, fireman, or biker might provide an interesting program. A high school student might bring a guitar and sing. Someone who makes stuffed toys might teach a group how to sew puppets. Smaller libraries, in particular, often use volunteers to do story programs. Volunteers, however, should always be given guidelines as to what the library wants done, and they should be supervised by staff to ensure program quality. Volunteers may also staff the area while librarians do programs. However they help, they should be recognized and thanked in some way. Volunteers should be truly willing and not coerced into doing programs for free.

Libraries should have a budget for programming to allow purchase of needed supplies and to pay for speakers and performer's fees, costs of audiovisual rentals, and other expenses. In libraries where the program budget is insufficient, Friends of the Library groups or parent-teacher organizations often will financially support activities which they see as beneficial to the library and the children.

In recent years, libraries have done a greater variety of programs than previously and experimented with many formats and ideas. To be successful, a program must first of all sound fun and interesting. If it sounds dull, children won't come. Programs which were successful 10 years ago may no longer draw children without some fresh approach. Sometimes, repackaging it with a new name, fresh publicity, and having it at a new time can make it more successful. It is also important that the program sound appropriate for the intended age group. For example, most eight-year-olds will think "story hour" is for little children even if it is storytelling for older children.

Programs must be on subjects that interest children, and librarians working with children need to be aware of children's interests as well as trends and fads. Giving a program or special event an unusual, eye- and ear-catching title can attract interest and attention. A program on food sounds dull, but call it "Mouse Stew and Popcorn Pie" or any humorous combination from stories, films, or activities in the program, and it sounds lively. Titles that are action-oriented are generally more successful than those that are descriptive. Titles that intrigue children will make them want to find out what it is all about.

Essential to successful programs is good publicity, especially in public libraries. Children cannot come if they don't know about it. Often publicity is done too little and too late. All publicity should stress that programs are free. In schools, having some idea ahead of time about what will happen in the media center can make children anticipate coming.

Also important in attracting people to programs is the library's programming reputation. Programs should be consistently well planned and of high quality. Children or parents who come to a poor program may not bother to come again.

The best planned program can fall victim to weather, conflicts with other community events or a special television program. All of these can't be avoided, but librarians can try to avoid conflicts by being aware of scheduled events and letting other groups and agencies know the library's calendar as early as possible. Sometimes programs that librarians think are great will fail with children. All librarians have failures. A program can work well in one location and fail in another. The timing may be wrong or the wrong age group targeted. Sometimes it just doesn't work as well as planned. However, it is better to try different approaches and fail than to never try anything new.

Sometimes libraries have a problem with an overwhelming response to certain programs. Too many children can be as much of a problem as too few. Activities may be impossible to do with too large a group. It may be necessary to offer a program at two separate times. Other alternatives are registration or handing out tickets to special events. Sometimes, registration and tickets make people feel a program must be really worthwhile and can actually be a technique to promote attendance.

Children of all ages can enjoy programs in libraries but generally not all together. Offer the appropriate program for the appropriate age group. Only occasionally will a program work for a wide age span. While attendance may be satisfactory, it may not satisfy all the children. Three-year-olds have very little in common with ten-year-olds or even seven-year-olds. Allowing preschoolers to attend programs advertised for older children will keep the older children away because it becomes in their eyes a program for babies. Older children attending programs for preschoolers can be disruptive because they are bored. Set age limits for programs and remain firm. Parents may complain when they cannot drop all the children off for a program, but other agencies and organizations such as schools, scouts, and churches set age limits for activities. Librarians may want occasionally to plan a program for the entire family but not make every program open to everyone. In the same way, school library media specialists may plan some special events only for certain grade levels but should try to have something special for each grade level during the year.

Librarians should try to include disabled children in programs. This will take special efforts in publicity and some accommodations by the library. These children have a right to participate in community activities but are often denied the opportunity. They often have special needs: an interpreter for the deaf for some programs, or objects that blind children can feel. Activities can often be adapted to make it possible for physically and mentally disabled children to participate. Few community organizations do this, and libraries can make an important contribution to children who may have few opportunities to attend events outside of school. It may be necessary to do special publicity and to make repeated efforts to attract these children because their families are not used to their being included.

In more urban areas, where activities are offered by recreation departments, museums, theaters, and a host of other organizations, the library may be competing for children's interest. In rural areas, children may have few opportunities for or-

ganized activities or cultural experiences. School library media specialists also need to be alert to what children are doing in the classroom. Developing working relationships with other agencies and organizations working with children will help librarians be better aware of what they are planning and let them know what the library is doing. This helps avoid duplication and scheduling conflicts. This is especially true for small-town public libraries, where the pool of children is limited. Best of all, working together helps ensure that the community offers a well-rounded variety of activities for children.

PROGRAM PLANNING

Planning is essential to good library programming. Each library should have an overall plan or policy for programming. Planning results in better organized, more purposeful programs, and fewer snags. The program policy should include the goals and objectives and outline criteria for deciding if a program will fit these goals and objectives. Writing goals and objectives may seem like a lot of unnecessary paperwork, but it is helpful in keeping programming on target, giving a basis for evaluation, and providing a basis for justifying programs to supervisors. It also prevents staff from moving away from activities that enhance the library's purposes into either quick entertainment programs with little substance or elaborate programs that have little connection with the library.

The programming plan should explain how programming will be related to books and literature and other materials in the library. The plan should also state the amount of staff time to be allocated for programming and how that time will be distributed among programming for various groups. For example, what percentage of the library's programming time should be allocated to preschoolers? How much time should be set aside for programming for organized groups such as child development centers, scout troops and school classes? In a school media center, the amount of time for special activities may be determined by class schedules and time needed for teaching of library skills. However, every effort should be made to allocate some time for special activities and programs for each grade level. Otherwise, it is easy to limit programming to areas of the population where the demand is greatest or to add more and more programming for groups and not have sufficient time for other job responsibilities. It also ensures that librarians don't allow other activities to push programming to the side.

The plan should include the amount of money available for program support such as supplies, film rentals, and fees for performers or special speakers. It should specify where programming will be held, and any limitations the library's facilities place on the types of activities offered, and the number of children who may attend. It should include criteria for evaluating programs. Finally, this general program plan should be approved by the supervisor or administrator to ensure support for what the children's librarian is trying to do through programming.

The general programming plan is used as a basis for an annual program plan. An annual plan does not tie librarians into a rigid schedule. Programs can be added or deleted as needed. A yearly plan allows librarians to budget time for programming and encourages analysis of what is being done and for whom; and it allows them to compare what they are doing with the overall goals. It also serves as a way of informing the administration of what is planned for the coming year, to request needed funds, and offers the opportunity for feedback.

The annual plan should state the goals and objectives for the year. Staff may have a new type of program they would like to try. They may want to try to reach an age group that has been ignored in the past. They may want to try to increase programming in branches, to reach more child development centers, or to stimulate reading by older children. Could last year's programming have been improved? Did the library do too much programming or too little? What worked and what didn't work? How will general library objectives affect the coming year's programming? Projects such as remodeling, retrospective conversion for computers, or special emphases can affect time and space available for programs. Finally, children should be included in the planning process. It is important to know what programs and activities they would enjoy.

With the goals, objectives, and budget in hand, librarians can develop program plans. In the annual plan, these may be general such as three eight-week sessions of preschool story hour, a month-long children's film festival, and summer reading activities. For a school library media center, they may include a special storytelling festival, a holiday celebration, or a student book review exchange network. Most libraries will have a combination of regular programs and one-time special events. Goals and objectives for each planned program or series will help ensure each program will be worth the time and effort. Fewer well-planned interesting programs are better than weekly programs hurriedly thrown together. Librarians should be realistic about how much time is available for programming. If the library has more than one person involved in doing programs, the supervisor should decide who will be responsible for each program or series. Tentatively schedule dates for each and estimate how much each program will cost.

Estimating program costs including staff costs will help determine the feasibility of a program idea and help justify time and activities involved. Figuring all program costs also lets the library see speaker and performance fees in relationship to costs for in-house produced programs. To calculate estimated program costs it is necessary to know the hourly wage for each staff member involved in programming. Multiply this by estimated planning and preparation time as well as actual programming time.

SAMPLE: Program Cost Tally Sheet

Calculating Program Costs		
Preschool Story Hours		
Three eight-week series (24 programs)		
	In-kind (staff)	Actual Expenditures
Staff		
Preparation: 24 hr. x $10/hr. =	$240	
Program: 24 hr. x $10/hr. = (30 min. program, 30 min. set up and clean up)	$240	
Publicity: 2 hr./series 6 hr. x $10/hr. =	$60	
Supplies and Printing =		$10
Publicity Printing and Supplies =		$40
Materials (books from library) =		$00
Total =	$540	
Total out-of-pocket expenditures =		$50
Estimated cost per program: $24.58 ([$540 + $50]/24)		
Estimated cost per program excluding staff $2.08 ($50/24)		

If transportation to a branch or other program location is required, include the time and costs for this.

SAMPLE: Program Planning Worksheet

Send news release on _____
Program title:_____
Theme (if applicable) _____
　　　Goals: 1._____
　　　Objectives: 1._____
　　　　　　　　　2._____
　　　　　　　　　3._____
　　　Objectives: 1._____
　　　　　　　　　2._____
　　　　　　　　　3._____
Target audience: Ages:____ Optimal group size:____
Date(s) and time: _____
Location(s): _____
Person responsible: _____
Other staff and volunteers needed: _____
Estimated planning and preparation time: ____
Program time: _____
Estimated staff costs: _____
Description of program: _____
_____

Materials needed: (check at left when have at hand or confirmed)

　　　Books:
　　　Films, filmstrips, or recordings:
　　　Display materials: _____
　　　Other materials and supplies: _____
　　　_____
　　　_____
　　　Samples and/or patterns made, if needed: ____
　　　_____
Total costs of materials and supplies: _____
Speaker/performer name: _____
　　　Address: _____
　　　Telephone: _____

Cost: ____ Confirmed: ____ Reminder call: ____
Thank you/payment sent: _____
Publicity (check when finished; attach samples): ____
　　　News release(s)_____
　　　Media Interview/talk show:_____
　　　Newspaper photographer and or media
　　　　contacted when desired: _____
　　　Posters:____ Flyers:____
　　　Plans for distribution: _____
　　　Room Arrangement: _____
　　　_____
　　　Equipment needed: _____
　　　Refreshments: What? How much? Pick up at?
　　　　Funded by?
　　　Reimbursement: _____
　　　_____

(This form is a compilation of forms used by different libraries.)

Once the overall programming policy and annual plan are complete, it is much easier to plan individual programs and series. The goals and objectives will already be laid out, leaving the programmer to plan activities to meet these. It is helpful to use a planning worksheet such as the one presented above, which includes a checklist of all the things that need to be done in preparation and provides accurate records of expenditures in dollars and time. An evaluation sheet should be completed after each program.

When the program involves a speaker or film, librarians should always plan an alternate program and have the resources ready in case of last-minute cancellations. Many children's librarians develop some emergency program plans and keep the needed materials at hand. A library never wants to send children away because something has gone wrong. Having a pre-planned program ready can also be useful to a staff member or substitute who must step in at the last minute if the librarian is ill or must be away from the library.

Program Evaluation Form

Title of Program: _____
Date: _____
Attendance: ____ Children: ____ Adults: ____
Age range of children attending: _____
Total staff time required for planning and
　　doing program: _____
Cost of staff: _____
Other costs (specify items): _____
_____
Total cost: _____
Description of program:
Participants' reactions:
How could the program be improved or
　changed:
Effectiveness of publicity:
Other comments:

Evaluation of programs should not be judged on attendance alone but should include assessment by staff of how the program went and evaluations or comments by participants. The person responsible should try to determine why it was or was not successful. Sometimes there is no clear reason. Rather than being discouraged when programs fail, librarians should try different scheduling and approaches and should be willing to admit when a particular program was a bad idea or not planned as well as it should have been.

Evaluations are important to help determine the effectiveness of programs and as guides for planning future programs. They provide important data for department reports and budgets. Using evaluation forms, librarians can determine which programs are effective and total costs and time spent on programming during any one year. Evaluation forms can be organized by type of program, age range served, and programs for the public versus programs for organized groups. A file of both planning and evaluation sheets is also very useful if staff wants to do similar programs again or for a new staff member to review what has been done and what has been successful. Evaluations also help identify when programming needs revision as indicated by slipping attendance or if planners feel programming is becoming stale.

BIBLIOGRAPHY

Materials on specific types of programs are listed in appropriate chapters.

Association for Library Service to Children. *Program Support Publications*. Chicago: American Library Association, 1980-1983.
  Nine short pamphlets, each of which focuses on one aspect of programming,

———. *Programming for Children with Special Needs*. Program Support Publications # 2. Chicago: American Library Association, 1981.

Bauer, Caroline Feller. *Celebrations; Read-Aloud Holiday and Theme Programs*. New York: H. W. Wilson, 1985.
  Stories, poems, activities, bibliographies.

———. *This Way to Books*. New York: H. W. Wilson, 1983.
  Book-related program and display ideas.

Kimmel, Margaret Mary. "Library — Program = Storehouse." *Top of the News* 32 (Fall 1975): 51-58.

Monson, Diane and DayAnn McClenathan. *Developing Active Readers: Ideas for Parents, Teachers, and Librarians*. Newark, DE: International Reading Association, 1979.

Paulin, Mary Ann. *Creative Uses of Children's Literature*. Hamden, CT: Library Professional Publications, 1982.

A Place Where I Belong: Serving Disabled Children in the Library. Vancouver, B.C.: Greater Vancouver Library Federation, 1986 (videotape).

Rayward, W. Boyd. "Programming in Public Libraries—Qualitative Evaluation." *Public Libraries* 24 (Spring 1985): 24-27.

Wilson, Patricia J. and Ann C. Kimzey. *Happenings: Developing Successful Programs for School Libraries*. Littleton, CO: Libraries Unlimited, 1987.

Programming for Preschool Children

Programming for preschool children has been a basic part of public library service to children for many years. It is an excellent way to introduce the library and books to young children and their families. Studies have shown that children who are read to regularly enjoy books more and are more interested in learning to read than children who lack this experience. Children who are exposed to books and different types of written communication are also more ready to learn to read.

The most common program for preschoolers is preschool story hour for children ages three to five. However, in recent years more libraries have begun to offer special story programs for toddlers as well as branching out into a greater variety of programming including craft times, and parent and child play sessions. More programs are designed for parents by both public and school libraries. Public libraries are also increasingly reaching out to day care and child development programs with programs and staff training.

PRESCHOOL STORY HOURS

The large increase in the number of young children in child care has forced public libraries to reassess their programming for preschool children. Even children with a parent at home often attend a morning nursery school program. As a result, many libraries find that there is less response to the traditional preschool story hour aimed at individual children brought by parents and an increased demand for programs for groups of children.

Children's librarians have become increasingly aware of the importance of reaching children in day care both through programs and training for those working with children. The content of programs offered to groups will not be that different, but programming for groups often requires more flexibility with ages and group size. Many libraries take programs to child care centers when it is not possible for the children to come to the library. In this case, it is very important for library staff to tell children each visit that they are from the library and to try to work out a way to circulate books to the centers visited.

School library media specialists use formats similar to preschool story hours with kindergarten and first-grade classes. As more school districts develop programs for preschool children, school librarians will have even more opportunities to use a story hour type of program.

Libraries should not try to combine an open preschool program for the public with one scheduled for a group. One or two children coming individually with parents will not feel comfortable in a group where the group dynamics is already fixed. Instead, schedule a separate series for children who come with parents even if the group is quite small. Good publicity and promotion will help recruit children for the program.

Whatever the group or location, the goal of preschool story programs should be to share and highlight books. Children listening to and participating in enjoyable stories and activities will learn and have a good time, but the primary purpose should not be to teach skills or concepts or to entertain. Fingerplays, body movement activities, songs, poetry, and simple creative drama allow for child-leader interaction and are good complements to books. Puppets, flannelboard stories, drawing stories, films, and other techniques can be used effectively in moderation. If too many different approaches are included in one program, books become the least exciting thing happening. Children may be more interested in what is coming next than in the stories. Young children are more actively responsive to books and other interactive activities. They tend to shift into a different gear with film, becoming either distracted or watching intently without reaction. Films or filmstrips should be used only when a particular item fits a program, will enrich the experience for children, or will act as a springboard to an activity or story.

In planning preschool story hours, begin by setting goals and objectives. Possible goals are introducing children to books and related activities, increasing interest in reading, increasing picture book circulation, and bringing young parents into the library. Objectives might include increasing the attendance at the program by a certain percentage and teaching three new fingerplays during the series.

Decide on the target group. For preschool story hour, it is generally three- to five-year-old children. For public programs, be firm with parents about age limits. Many parents believe their children are advanced, but when the library makes an exception for one person, it must make it for all.

Programs for public groups scheduled on a weekly basis for a specified time period are better than biweekly or monthly programs for younger children. Regularity allows librarians to build on the previous week's program and the children to get accustomed to the routine. Irregular scheduling also makes it more likely parents will forget about it. Some libraries offer this program every week. Others offer several series of six to eight weeks during the year. The latter gives staff planning time and both staff and children a break in the routine. Attendance is often better because parents realize it is available for a limited time only. On the other hand, some librarians feel children only begin to settle into the program after six weeks.

In general, morning is the best time of the day for younger children. However, libraries now often find an afternoon session is better attended because children who attend half-day preschool programs are home in the afternoon. Some libraries have held evening "bedtime" story hours, both as a novelty and to try to meet the needs of working parents. These have often had a mixed response. Working parents are usually tired and busy in the evenings. This type of novelty program is best planned as a short series rather than as a regular program, unless there is consistent demand.

Libraries often register children for public preschool story hour to limit group size. Generally this works best when programs are done in series. Even where too many children is not a problem, registration often increases the regularity of attendance because it makes parents feel the program is special. Knowing the same children are coming each week makes it easier to build on previous programs. It also gives the library a record of the parent's name, address, and telephone number. There are always some children who don't come, so if a group of 15 to 20 children is desired, register about 25 children. With groups of children it is essential to have a schedule of when they are coming. Groups of children arriving unexpectedly at a public story hour can make the group unwieldy in size.

Scheduling for groups is dictated by the number of groups being served, distances, and the group's needs. Some libraries feel a monthly visit gives continuity to library service; others prefer to do a series of several weeks for groups and then schedule different groups for another series.

If possible, hold the program away from library traffic. If there is no meeting room, choose an open area and arrange it so that the librarian and books are the center of attention. A low table to display books with an object or simple display related to the theme will help create a mood. Children do best sitting flat on the floor on carpet or carpet squares rather than sitting in chairs. It makes it easier to get them up and moving about for stretching and other activities. The person doing the program should sit on a chair or low stool so that the children behind the front row can see the books. When the children arrive, take time to arrange them so that all can see. A squared-off pie shape is ideal. If children are allowed to sit too close to the person reading stories or at their side, they have a difficult time seeing the pictures.

If the library is doing programs out of the library, it is necessary to adapt to the facility.

Children should be in a comfortable and intimate arrangement.

Librarians should plan by series or several weeks in advance. They need to select the books and set them aside, so they are available when needed, and choose fingerplays and related activities. Three or four books or stories, fingerplays, songs, and a poem or rhyme will make up a 30-minute program. Some libraries like to plan by themes such as animals, trains, spring, or feelings. Others prefer a mixed-bag program. A mixture of both types is fine.

Choose books with good, clear pictures that can be seen well from a distance. Books should have a good balance of pictures and text. Preschoolers will not sit for a very long story with few pictures. Some stories that work well one on one can be too long or slow moving for a group. Stories should be read as the author wrote them, not simplified or abridged. Books which are too long should be avoided so there won't be a need to shorten them. Children can enjoy these when they are older.

A variety of art styles, lengths, and tempos is desirable. Four stories all in rhyme or books all by the same illustrator can make for a dull program. Variety in content is also important. The mainstays for preschool programs are story books, preferably with a clear plot, that tell the story, and then end. Books that encourage child participation, such as concept books, alphabet and number books, and other books which invite child response are good. Books that don't tell a story but explore a feeling or idea have less immediate child appeal: one in a program is enough. Simple storytelling without books or visual aids can also be included if stories chosen are short and uncomplicated. Simple folktales, with which children may be already familiar, are good choices. Flannelboard and drawing stories are always popular with children.

In getting ready for preschool story hour make time to become familiar with the stories. Practice reading the texts aloud several times to become familiar with the words and rhythm. Learn any repetitive phrasing which adds flavor to the story. It is not necessary to memorize texts, but comfortable familiarity with them allows the reader to maintain eye contact and create a feeling of sharing the story with the children. Think about what to say to introduce and end each story. Reading the title and author or talking briefly about the theme

is sufficient. Those just beginning to do story hours can try recording themselves on a tape recorder to listen to reading voice and pace. Reading into a mirror will show how to handle the books.

Books should be held with pages facing the children. By holding the book with one hand firmly in the middle either at the top or bottom and using the other hand to turn pages, it can be done smoothly. Avoid crossing an arm over the pictures as pages are turned. Practice doing this until it is smooth and natural. Turning a picture book away from the children to read and back to the children to show pictures disrupts the flow of the story.

Read with expression but without exaggerated or overly dramatized voices. A slight voice variation between characters is more effective than forcing voices into very high or low pitches to try to imitate animal and other voices. Exaggerated voices tend to focus attention on the reader rather than on the story. Read slowly to allow children time to enjoy each picture. Use the words as written by the author who carefully thought out each word. Don't substitute more common words for those in the text. Children enjoy the sounds of words and learn vocabulary by context. It is not necessary to explain most words or ideas before reading the story unless understanding a particular word is crucial to the story.

Questions or comments during the story can be disruptive to the rest of the group. Responses should be kept short and children should be encouraged to wait until the end for any discussion. Avoid asking children questions during the story. After a story keep any discussion short. The purpose of story hour is to share literature, and not to check comprehension. Be prepared for little reaction from some children or to certain stories. Stories that don't trigger immediate reaction may make a strong impression that stays with children but needs time to come out. Don't ask if they liked the story, because this can stop their thinking about it.

Many people like to begin with a fingerplay or song to help children settle down. By using a short activity between each story, children have an opportunity to move a little and to break mentally from one story to another. Very energizing activities such as games in the middle of a program can break the mood. More active activities are better at the end of the program. Encourage parents and teachers to allow children a few minutes to look at books and to borrow books to read at home or school. Providing a list of stories and activities and some further suggestions of books to share can be helpful to both parents and teachers.

Good preparation will minimize problems during programs. Any disruptions such as children becoming distracted or needing to use the bathroom should be handled as smoothly as possible. Often, reading one or two sentences directly at disruptive children will bring them back into the story. Obvious attempts at attention getting should be ignored. Children at this age often behave better without parents around, and usually parents of three- to five-year-old children do not stay with the children. Encourage them to browse or read a magazine during the program. A parents' day once during a series of programs allows parents to see what the children are doing during story time. Teachers who bring groups should also be encouraged to sit back away from the group and to let the librarian handle the children during the program. A teacher constantly correcting children can be very distracting.

TODDLER STORY PROGRAMS

Toddler story hours are proving to be popular and successful. They are generally offered for children aged anywhere from eighteen months to just before three years. While the format of the program is not substantially different from that of the preschool story hour, it is not just a watered down story hour. Toddler programs are offered for the parent and children together. Toddlers are not generally ready to sit in a group without a parent or familiar adult present. The parents act as supporters, helping their children feel comfortable and participating with them in activities. As children hear stories and learn fingerplays, the parents are also learning about reading to children and some simple activities to do with them at home.

Most libraries have found that making toddler programs a shared parent-child activity is the best approach. They insist that a parent come with each child, except in the case of twins. For this reason, they are often not done for day care and other groups. With toddlers, a small group of 10 to 15 or even smaller is the maximum desired. Registration may be necessary to control group size and to encourage continuity of attendance. The length of the program is usually about 20 minutes, which is

all or more than toddlers can sit. The program is somewhat more informal than the traditional preschool story hour in that parents are encouraged not to worry about their children wandering, standing up, or being distracted, but instead to let the children pay attention when they want to as long as they don't disturb other children. To do successful toddler programs, the librarian needs to be able to tolerate a little side activity during stories and to be very flexible.

In choosing books for toddler programs, select short stories with very simple plots. Board books and simple concept books are also good sources of material. Plan no more than three books with fingerplays and songs in between. With fingerplays, use the same ones numerous times so the children will begin to learn them. Since parents are encouraged to read and do activities at home, provide them with a list of books, fingerplays, and songs presented.

OTHER PROGRAMS FOR PRESCHOOLERS

The philosophy underlying many programs for preschoolers is to provide parent-child activities that parents can use or adapt for home. Some libraries have begun to incorporate simple craft activities into preschool story hours or to offer craft times as a separate program. This is good as long as it does not take away from the emphasis on books, which are the library's unique contribution to the community. Craft or art activities should be designed so that they can be done by the child with help. Too often crafts for young children consist of their adding a final touch to a pretty thing primarily made by adults.

Libraries, especially those with toy collections, may offer parent-child play sessions where parents are taught to use a toy creatively with their children and to help their children learn through play. These may be done by staff or by other community resources with expertise in child development. Other areas of programming which benefit preschoolers include programs on parenting skills, reading to children, and children's literature and other topics. Many libraries also offer in-service training for teachers in early childhood programs. These will be discussed in Chapter 15, "Services to Parents and Other Adults."

FIGURE 5. Toddler story time provides both parents and toddlers exposure to books, fingerplays, and songs. (Richland County [SC] Public Library)

BIBLIOGRAPHY

Association for Library Service to Children. *Programming for Very Young Children.* Program Support Publications #1. Chicago: American Library Association, 1980.

Bauer, Caroline Feller. *Creative Storytelling Techniques.* Chicago: American Library Association, 1979 (videocassette).

———. *Handbook for Storytellers.* Chicago: American Library Association, 1977.

———. *Programming for Three- to Five-Year-Olds.* Program Support Publications #8, Chicago: American Library Association, 1983.

Carlson, Ann D. *Early Childhood Literature Sharing Programs in Libraries.* Hamden, CT: Library Professional Publications, 1985.

Cromwell, Liz, Dixie Hibner, and John R. Faitel. *Finger Frolics; Over 250 Fingerplays for Children from Three Years.* Rev. ed. Livonia, MI: Partner Press, 1983.

Foster, Joanna, comp. *How to Conduct Effective Picture Book Programs; A Handbook.* Westchester, NY: Westchester Library System, 1967.
  Written to accompany the film *The Pleasure Is Mutual.*

Grayson, Marion. *Let's Do Fingerplays.* Washington, DC: Robert B. Luce, 1962.

Greene, Ellin. "Early Childhood Centers: Three Models." *School Library Journal* 30 (Feb 1984): 21-27.

Johnson, Ferne, ed. *Start Early for an Early Start: You and the Young Child.* Chicago: American Library Association, 1976.

Kewish, Nancy. "South Euclid's Pilot Project for Two-Year-Olds and Parents." *School Library Journal* 25 (Mar 1979): 93-98.

Lima, Carolyn. *A to Zoo; Subject Access to Children's Picture Books.* 2nd ed. New York: Bowker, 1986.
  Useful bibliography for identifying books by theme or subject.

Mallett, Jerry and Marion R. Bartoh. *Stories to Draw.* Hagerstown, MD: Freline, 1982.

Moore, Vardine. *The Preschool Story Hour.* Metuchen, NJ: Scarecrow Press, 1972.

Nichols, Judy. *Storytimes for Two-Year-Olds.* Chicago: American Library Association, 1987.

Peterson, Carolyn Sue and Brenny Hall. *Story Programs: A Source Book of Materials.* Metuchen, NJ: Scarecrow Press, 1980.

The Pleasure Is Mutual; How to Conduct Effective Picture Book Programs. Connecticut Films, 1967 (16mm film).

Polette, Nancy. *E Is for Everybody; A Manual for Bringing Fine Picture Books into the Hands and Hearts of Children.* Metuchen, NJ: Scarecrow Press, 1982.

Ring a Ring O' Roses; Stories, Games and Fingerplays for Preschool Children. Flint, MI: Flint Public Library, 1977.

Sharing Literature with Children. Orlando, FL: Orlando Public Library, 1975 (16mm film).

Sierra, Judy. *The Flannel Board Storytelling Book.* New York: H. W. Wilson, 1987.

Sitarz, Paula. *Picture Book Story Hours: From Birthdays to Bears.* Littleton, CO: Libraries Unlimited, 1987.

Smardo, Frances A. and John F. Curry. *What Research Tells Us about Story Hours and Receptive Language.* Dallas, TX: Dallas Public Library, 1982.

Thomas, James and Marilyn Vaughn, eds. *Sharing Books with Young Children.* Minneapolis, MN: T. S. Denison, 1987.

Young, Diana. "Service to Children in Groups." *Public Libraries* 25 (Fall 1986): 100-104.
Report of Hennepin County Library Task Force on library service to children in groups.

11

Storytelling, Puppetry, and Creative Drama

STORYTELLING

Storytelling is the art of sharing stories by telling rather than reading them. Storytelling is a historic part of the cultures of most countries serving as a way of passing on events, values and customs from one generation to another. It was a major source of family and community entertainment. During the twentieth century in the Western world, its use declined with the growth of mass formal education, radio, television, and other forms of entertainment. During this period, libraries continued to tell stories to children, and it has been a long-standing and traditional part of library programming.

In recent years, there has been a great resurgence of interest in storytelling outside of libraries. A number of people make their living once again as travelling storytellers. There is a burgeoning number of storytelling festivals through the country, some of which are aimed as much or more for adults as for children. However, libraries remain one of the places where children can hear storytelling on a regular basis. Because of its connections with literature, it is an important way of sharing literature with children. It is also a good way to share the past and present with children.

Many books can help librarians learn more about selecting stories and storytelling techniques as well as how to use storytelling effectively in the library. One of the best is *Storytelling: Art and Technique*, written by Augusta Baker and Ellin Greene (1977). It inspires people to want to tell stories and provides practical suggestions based on years of experience. Films and recordings featuring storytellers can also be helpful.

Storytelling is one of the best ways to teach children the pure joy of a story. There is no book or other object between the storyteller and the children, allowing the storyteller to maintain full eye contact with the children. Good storytellers use both voice and body language subtly to express mood and pace in the story. Children benefit from listening without visual aids. They learn to imagine their own visual impressions and to listen and absorb only through their ears. Some librarians feel that children today do not enjoy just listening to a story. When you see a group of children listening to a good storyteller, you know this is not true.

The process of storytelling involves selecting, learning, and telling stories. Each part of the process is important. Probably the best way to choose a story is to hear one you want to tell. Listening to storytellers in person, on records and on tapes are excellent ways to hear a variety of stories and storytellers. Storytelling festivals provide opportunities to hear numerous storytellers and stories. Books of folk and fairy tales are a rich source of stories as are myths, legends, and fables. Original stories, often called literary tales, by authors such as Hans Christian Andersen, Eleanor Farjeon, Walter de la Mare, Joan Aiken, and many others are another source. Storytellers can also use stories from a children's novel if there are complete and distinct episodes.

Selecting a story can in itself be a difficult process. Reading or listening to many stories may be necessary to find those the storyteller really wants to learn. Plots should be straightforward without subplots and diversions unless they really add to the story. Characters should be believable. Action should begin early in the story. Plots with suspense, a good climax, and a satisfying ending will hold listeners' attention better than stories which have lots of description and little action. Stories which draw clear pictures with words will hold listeners' attention. Rhythm and repetitive phrases add interest and are helpful in learning the stories. Stories also need to be suitable to the intended audience. There may be numerous versions of a story as it has been retold by different people, and it is helpful to read several versions before choosing one to learn. Versions that are faithful to the original are best. Watered down or softened language or plot diminish the effect of the story. Folk tale indexes and bibliographies can help in locating stories on particular subjects or themes.

Beginning storytellers can choose a story that is short and familiar. By choosing a well-known folktale for younger children such as *Caps for Sale* or *The Gingerbread Boy*, they will find they almost know it just from having read it to children. Different storytellers use different learning methods. Some people like to visualize a story in detailed pictures like the sequences of a motion picture. Others learn by logically reconstructing the story in their minds. For others, concentrating on the sounds of words and their rhythm helps them to learn the story. Typing or writing out the story can help some people begin to imprint it on their minds. Reading the story onto a cassette and playing it back over and over while driving or doing routine tasks is another good method. Whatever method works well, it is essential that the plot and sequence of events be completely learned.

Whether storytellers learn the words as written or tell the story in their own words is a matter of choice, but it is important to retain the style of the original and to memorize any rhymes and phrases that repeat themselves throughout the story. Literary tales should be learned and told as written because the language used is part of the character of the story. Because of the necessity to memorize words as written and to preserve the cadence and style of the author, these are considered more difficult to tell. Any editing must be done with great care so as not to alter the author's style or intent.

Storytellers should allow plenty of time to learn a story well. They must get beyond learning the sequence and words to conveying the desired mood and feeling through voice, pace, and effective use of pauses. Pace is particularly important since nervousness can cause storytellers to speed up, giving the impression they can't wait to get through the story. Before telling a story to a group, storytellers should have told it to themselves numerous times so that the words flow naturally, and they feel very comfortable with it. Family and friends can make good practice audiences.

It is easy never to find time to learn stories in the press of other responsibilities. Select a date or special program well in advance to tell a new story and work on the story gradually. Beginning storytellers should not attempt to learn too many new stories in a short period or they may be overwhelmed.

Storytellers often don't feel good about a story the first time they tell it. As they become more comfortable with it, the story usually becomes more enjoyable to tell. Storytellers should try to tell any story they learn as often as they can. A story told one time is easily forgotten, but a story told again and again will remain stored in the memory so that it can be used months or even years later with only a little polishing or refreshing.

Storytelling is habit forming. It is often difficult to do at first but, as new storytellers become more confident and experience the response of the people who listen to the stories, they will most likely want to do it more often. The process of storytelling can be summed up with three "L" words:

Love it—choose stories to learn that you love;
Learn it—learn it so that you can tell it with
    confidence;
Live it—make it your own by telling it often
    and giving it your personal imprint through
    your telling.

Storytelling can be used in library programs in many different ways. Traditionally, many public libraries have had story hours for older children. Today, this often does not attract many school-age children, who tend to think of stories as something for little children. However, because older children enjoy stories when they have the opportunity to listen to them, storytelling should be part of programs as often as possible. Storytelling can be a part of a program along with crafts, book talks, films, puppets, and other activities. Public librarians can tell stories as part of school and other tours and on school visits. They can include a simple story told without a book in a preschool

FIGURE 6. Storytelling festivals are an increasingly popular way to showcase the art of storytelling. This one in Columbia, South Carolina, honors Augusta Baker.

story hour. A family storytelling night can be offered as a special program. School librarians can incorporate storytelling into class activities in the library. They can tell stories related to what children are studying. Hearing a story from Russia or one about a turtle can enrich units on these subjects. Some libraries teach children how to tell stories and then hold a storytelling festival or contest to let them show off their new skills. Older children could tell their stories to younger ones.

Storytelling is also a natural activity for community festivals. Short stories are best, since people tend to wander in and out and won't stay in one place for a long time. More and more libraries are sponsoring storytelling festivals, inviting public and school librarians and other storytellers to participate. This would be an excellent project for school and public libraries to cosponsor for the community.

PUPPETRY

Children love puppets. They like to watch, use, talk to, cuddle, and generally enjoy them. Puppets are magic and wonderful. A puppet is not alive until someone brings it to life. Any inanimate object can become a puppet, and a puppet can be made with almost anything. The scope of puppetry is limited only by imagination and the ability to give vitality to the puppets.

Libraries can use puppets and their appeal to bring literature to children in new and different ways. The most formal and probably the most popular of these is the puppet show of a story, song, or skit. Puppets can also be used more informally to assist at story hours and other programs. Some libraries also set up a puppet corner where children can play and put on impromptu plays when they are in the library. Others check puppets out to children.

FIGURE 7. A puppet corner encourages children to explore puppetry and put on impromptu plays. (Kershaw County [SC] Library)

Another good way to bring puppetry into the library is to have a series of classes on making and using puppets for school-age children. In a school this may be done by a teacher as a classroom project, and the library can supply books and other materials on puppetry and ideas for plays. It may also be done as a library unit. A public library can plan a class of several sessions. Registration may be necessary to ensure a manageable size group. Puppets that are simple and don't need much sewing such as paper bag, paper plate, box, and sock puppets, are good choices for beginners. Children will get an opportunity to make some puppets and to get experience using them informally and in a play. From a series of classes such as this, some of the children may want to put on a show for other children, and a few may be interested enough to form a school or public library puppetry club.

For library use, puppets can be purchased or made from paper, cloth, papier-mache, wax, wood, and almost anything else. Most puppets fall into one of several types. Finger puppets are small puppets designed for use on the fingers. They work well for use with small groups. Children find them easy to manipulate. Some glove puppets which have a different character on each finger are an adaptation of the finger puppet. Hand puppets are any puppets manipulated by the hand. One type uses one or two fingers in the head and a finger in each arm. The puppeteer can move head and hands making it relatively easy to give the puppet personality. Mouth puppets, best exemplified by the Muppets, are also hand puppets, but the movement is restricted to opening and shutting the mouth unless rods are added for limb control. These puppets can have lots of expression. Rod puppets are controlled by a rod attached to the body of the puppet. They may be stick puppets with a single rod, or they may have separate rods attached to the hand or other parts of the body where movement is desired. Marionettes are hung with a string or strings and operated from above. They are more difficult to manipulate when they have multiple strings, which also give them a great range of movement. Marionettes require a different style of stage and require more skill to use well. Many of the top professional puppeteers use marionettes, but they are less common in library productions. Single or two-string puppets can be used effectively with stories, and it is easy to get them to walk with personality.

To use puppets informally in a preschool story hour or other program, a stage and props are not needed. Some librarians like to use a puppet to welcome children to story hour and to introduce stories. Puppets can also be used occasionally for a special poem or in conjunction with a special story. Used in this way, a puppet takes on the role of a friend who may talk with the librarian and children. Sometimes the puppet may be shy and willing to whisper only in the librarian's ear. Using puppets this way can be a great addition, but one must be careful not to let the puppet take over so that it becomes more important than the stories.

In a puppet show, the puppets become actors. Puppets are needed for each character in the story or skit, although simple costume changes can allow one puppet to play several parts. A stage is also necessary, but it can be anything from a table turned on its side or a refrigerator box to a more permanent stage. Stage plans can be found in many books, and there are commercial stages available as well. Before building or purchasing a stage, consider the library's needs carefully. If the stage will be used throughout a system, at outreach activities, or in different classrooms, portability is essential. Lighting and a sound system will make programs seem more professional.

Puppet plays may be based on children's stories or be original stories. Puppet plays can be found in books and in magazines such as *Plays*, or can be adapted from a children's book or story collection. However, librarians must be careful not to use copyrighted material without permission. In a library setting, it is important that puppetry enhance the library's role in interpreting literature to children. In adapting stories, stay close to the original plot and use original dialogue wherever possible. The insertion of too many jokes and other diversions can bring a lot of laughs, but these can take over the plot and reduce the impact of the story.

In making or purchasing puppets, begin with ones that can be used in numerous ways. Basic people puppets can become any human character with a change of costume, a new wig, and accessories. Animals can be used in people roles very effectively with proper costuming. Children love animals playing people. Think of all the wonderful children's books written on this premise. A basic collection of puppets would include several people puppets and a few animals that can be used in a number of plays. Special characters can be added as needed. Libraries beginning to use puppets should think about plays the staff wants to do before buying or making puppets.

Whether puppets are made or purchased, they are only as effective as the way they are used. The most beautiful puppet will be lifeless if not given life by its manipulator, and a lowly paper bag puppet can become a lively creature. Make the puppets as attractive and convincing as possible, but do not put so much time into the puppet making that there is not enough time for rehearsing and polishing the performance. Do not hesitate to begin with simple, homemade puppets of paper and other scrap materials. The personality the puppeteers create for the puppets will make them seem real and alive. There are lots of wonderful books on puppet construction which include patterns and specific instructions. Many soft toy patterns can be adapted to puppets.

Once the puppets are ready, it is important to bring them to life effectively. Making them move realistically is important because puppets can look stiff and awkward if poorly manipulated. Keep puppets standing straight, not tilting forward or back or against the stage. Nonspeaking puppets should be still when other puppets are talking or moving. Move fingers, wrist, and arms to give the puppet meaningful motion. Practice with a mirror or use videotape to see what effect different movement provides. Puppet voices should be clear, loud enough to be heard, fit the character, and be distinct from the other characters in the play. Good movement and voices make for believable characterization.

Voices can be done live with each performance or taped ahead of time. With live voices, the show can quickly adapt to the audience and respond to their comments and reactions. Taped productions set the pace for the puppeteers, but they free them to concentrate on puppet manipulations. This makes it easier when puppeteers change at different performances or when a puppet show is sent to a branch or school. Taping allows use of voices suitable to the characters and sound effects can be added at the time of recording. Both methods have their supporters, and libraries need to decide which method works best for them.

CREATIVE DRAMA

Creative drama is improvisational drama in which children are guided to express themselves. It is a special kind of play that involves imitation, imagination, make-believe, and role playing. It is a wonderful activity for children because it allows them to express their feelings openly, stretch their imaginations and thoughts in new ways, move and use their bodies to convey meaning, and interact with other children in a different way. Creative expression is very important in a child's development. Through movement and drama, children are able to express feelings and thoughts they cannot verbalize. When they become truly involved, they lose self-consciousness and really let themselves go to express themselves with the activity in ways that can contribute to their self-image. Since many of the activities involve working together, children also learn how to work cooperatively. Creative drama also fits beautifully into library activities because it can often be based on books, stories, poetry, or films and can, therefore, be another way to share literature with children. School librarians may be able to also use it to extend topics in the curriculum.

Creative dramatics in its pure form is done as a separate class designed with activities to help children learn how to do improvisational drama. In *Creative Dramatics in the Library* (1976), Nancy Pereira explains a formal creative drama program in a library. Some libraries may want to consider this as a program series with either staff or a person experienced in drama leading the group. Since regular attendance is important to build on skills learned, this would need to be a program where registration is required and the group size limited. There are numerous books available with suggested exercises and activities.

Creative drama can also be incorporated into other library programs. Libraries doing preschool story hours are already using creative drama in a very basic form. Fingerplays and action rhymes involve children in acting out a verse and a story. Many action rhymes are whole body activities, such as children melting like a snowman, walking like animals, or becoming a flower. Children sing songs or listen to music that involves them in creative movement. These are all creative drama activities. They extend the story or poem and help children to use their imagination.

Older children are capable of putting more intensity and deeper thought into what they imagine if the setting and mood involve and encourage them to take the activity seriously. Creative drama can be used in response to or as an introduction to a film or story, or as an independent activity related to a program theme. *Puppetry and Creative Dramatics in Storytelling* (1980) by Connie Champlin suggests ways to incorporate dramatic activities into storytelling by getting children to participate in the telling through such activities as repeating phrases and doing sound effects. There are ideas for sequence games which are circle games that can be based on books or subjects. She describes activity and narrative pantomimes, making group creations, and other drama activities any librarian can use. The activities can be done with or without puppetry as well.

To involve children successfully in creative drama, the leaders must lose their inhibitions and be willing to participate in the drama activities. Librarians will find that not only is creative drama something children enjoy, it is also an effective way to add to the experiences library programs provide for children.

BIBLIOGRAPHY

Storytelling

Association for Library Service to Children. *Storytelling: Readings, Bibliographies, Resources.* Chicago: American Library Association, 1978.

Baker, Augusta. "Storytelling." Prelude, Series 1. New York: Children's Book Council, 1975 (cassette).

Baker, Augusta and Ellin Greene. *Storytelling: Art and Technique.* New York: Bowker, 1977.

Breneman, Lucille N. and Bren Breneman. *Once Upon a Time: A Storytelling Handbook.* Chicago: Nelson-Hall, 1983.

Bryant, Sara Cone. *How to Tell Stories to Children.* New York: Houghton Mifflin, 1905.

De Wit, Dorothy. *Children's Faces Looking Up: Program Building for the Storyteller.* Chicago: American Library Association, 1979.

Greene, Ellin and George Shannon. *Storytelling; A Selected Annotated Bibliography.* New York: Garland, 1986.

Livo, Norma J. and Sandra A. Rietz. *Storytelling: Process and Practice.* Littleton, CO: Libraries Unlimited, 1986.

———. *Storytelling Activities.* Littleton, CO: Libraries Unlimited, 1987.

MacDonald, Margaret. *Twenty Tellable Tales: Audience Participation Folktales for the Beginning Storyteller.* New York: H. W. Wilson, 1986.

Miller, Theresa, comp. *An Anthology of Audience Participation Stories and How to Tell Them!* Cambridge, MA: Yellow Moon Press, 1988.

Pellowski, Anne. *The Story Vine: A Source Book of Unusual and Easy-to-Tell Stories from Around the World.* New York: Macmillan, 1984.

———. "Using Folklore as an Introduction to Other Cultures." Prelude, Series 2. New York: Children's Book Council, 1976 (cassette).

———. *The World of Storytelling.* New York: Bowker, 1977.

Sawyer, Ruth. *The Way of the Storyteller.* New York: Viking, 1962.

Shedlock, Marie. *The Art of the Storyteller.* 3rd ed. New York: Dover, 1951.

Stories Everywhere. National Association for the Preservation and Perpetuation of Storytelling, 1982 (videotape).

There's Something about a Story. Public Library of Dayton and Montgomery County with Connecticut Films, 1971 (16mm film).

Wilson, Jane E. *The Story Experience.* Metuchen, NJ: Scarecrow Press, 1979.

Young, Diana. "Storytelling Festivals." *Public Libraries* 26 (Winter 1987): 176-178.

Ziskind, Sylvia. *Telling Stories to Children.* New York: H. W. Wilson, 1976.

Bibliographies of Stories

Carnegie Library of Pittsburgh. *Stories to Tell to Children: A Selected List.* 8th ed. Edited by Laura E. Cathon et al. Pittsburgh, PA: University of Pittsburgh Press, 1974.

Eastman, Mary Huse. *Index to Fairy Tales, Myths and Legends.* 2nd ed. Boston: Faxon, 1926. First Supplement, 1937; Second Supplement, 1950.

Ireland, Norma Olin. *Index to Fairy Tales, 1949-1972: Including Folklore, Legends, and Myths in Collections.* Westwood, MA: Faxon, 1973. (Fourth Supplement, 1973-1977, 1985.)

MacDonald, Margaret. *The Storyteller's Sourcebook: A Subject, Title and Motif Index to Folktale Collections for Children.* New York: Neal-Schumann, 1982.

New York Public Library. *Stories: A List of Stories to Tell and Read Aloud.* 7th ed. New York: New York Public Library, 1977.

Puppetry

Anderson, Benny E. *Let's Start a Puppet Theatre.* New York: Van Nostrand, 1973.

Batchelder, Marjorie. *The Puppet Theatre Handbook.* New York: Harper, 1947.

Champlin, Connie. *Puppetry and Creative Dramatics in Storytelling.* Austin, TX: Nancy Renfro Studios, 1980.

Champlin, Connie and Nancy Renfro. *Storytelling with Puppets.* Chicago: American Library Association, 1985.

Currell, David. *The Complete Book of Puppet Theatre.* Totawa, NJ: Barnes and Noble Books, 1987.

Engler, Larry and Carol Fijan. *Making Puppets Come Alive.* New York: Taplinger, 1973.

Freericks, Mary. *Creative Puppetry in the Classroom.* Rowayton, CT: New Plays, 1979.

Kampman, Lothar. *Creating with Puppets.* New York: Van Nostrand, 1972.

Renfro, Nancy. *A Puppet Corner in Every Library.* Austin, TX: Nancy Renfro Studios, 1978.

———. *Puppetry and the Art of Story Creation.* Austin: TX: Nancy Renfro Studios, 1979.

———. *Puppets for Play Production.* New York: Funk and Wagnalls, 1969.

Renfro, Nancy and Ann Weiss Schwalb. "Show Centers for Library Media Centers: Establishing Puppet Performance Centers in the Library." *School Library Media Activities Monthly* 2 (Jan 1986): 29-36.

Richter, Dorothy. *Fell's Guide to Hand Puppets.* New York: F. Fell, 1970.

Tichenor, Tom. *Tom Tichenor's Puppets.* Nashville, TN: Abingdon, 1971.

Creative Drama

Association for Library Service to Children. *Programming with Interpretive Activities.* Program Support Publication #6. Chicago: American Library Association, 1982.

Carlson, Bernice Wells. *Let's Pretend It Happened to You.* Nashville, TN: Abingdon, 1973.

———. *Picture That!* Nashville, TN: Abingdon, 1977.

Champlin, Connie. *Puppetry and Creative Dramatics in Storytelling.* Austin, TX: Nancy Renfro Studios, 1980.

Fitzgerald, Burdette S. *World Tales for Creative Dramatics and Storytelling.* New York: Prentice-Hall, 1962.

King, Nancy. *Giving Form to Feeling.* New York: Drama Book Specialists, 1975.
Stimulating ideas for movement and creative activities.

Nobleman, Roberta. *Fifty Projects for Creative Dramatics.* New York: New Plays for Children, 1971.

Pereira, Nancy. *Creative Dramatics in the Library.* 2nd ed. Rowayton, CT: New Plays, 1966.

Reid, V. "Bringing Books to Life Through Drama." Prelude, Series 1. New York: Children's Book Council, 1975 (cassette).

Sikes, Geraldine. *Creative Dramatics, An Art for Children.* New York: Harper, 1958.

Ward, Winifred. *Playmaking with Children.* New York: Appleton Century, 1967.

Using Nonprint Media in Library Activities

The availability and variety of nonprint materials in our society has grown tremendously. They have great appeal to many children, and libraries have used them extensively. These materials can be used in ways that expand children's experiences, understandings, or creativity. Too often, however, they are used for quick programming or simple entertainment. Used without careful planning, they may do little but encourage children to be passive receivers of stimuli. By using them to enhance children's experiences and learning, libraries can help children become actively involved in film, music, the arts, play, and new technologies so that they can become a tool rather than merely a source of easy entertainment. By giving children the opportunity to see, listen to, feel, and touch the best of what is available, libraries can give them the opportunity to learn to be selective users of these materials.

FILM AND VIDEOTAPE

Film, whether on 16mm film or on videotape, is a medium that captures children's attention and has great potential for creative use in programming. Children are very visually oriented and enjoy film. They can be entertained and inspired by it. Film can educate and inform children by showing them new places, unusual jobs, or what something looks like very close up or very far away. They can learn about different people and life styles and gain new perspectives about the world. In schools, films can be used to teach facts and increase understanding of topics in the curriculum by giving children an alive and intimate view of subject. When good quality film is shown, it can also help children develop critical viewing skills and learn what makes a good or a bad film. In today's visually oriented society, visual literacy is a necessary skill. Children need to understand visual messages and themes and to see how the film is put together and what the filmmaker was trying to accomplish. Film can also encourage reading. Children will often ask for books of films they have seen. In public libraries, film can also be a good way to attract children who might not attend a book program.

Film can be used in children's programming in many ways. It can be used as one element in a program. A film related to a theme can be used in a story hour. It can be used in a mixed media program as a lead-in to a craft, movement, or drama activity. Libraries often have film programs showing several films related in some way or a single longer film. Libraries may sponsor children's film festivals to spotlight outstanding children's films. In schools, curriculum-related films are used more in the classrooms, but the library can use other films for its activities and encourage teachers to use them in creative ways.

It is important to have goals and objectives for film programs so that they are planned in a way that will benefit the library and also provide children with a positive experience. Programs should be planned and publicized for a specific age range so appropriate films can be used. In planning a film program, plan no more than 30 minutes for preschoolers. For children six and older, the program can run 45 to 60 minutes or longer if a feature film is shown. Themes can be helpful in making the films fit together to make a unified program, not just a series of films. Likewise, when films are incorporated into a program with other activities, the films and activities should make a whole.

One difficulty with using film can be getting the desired titles at the desired time. Often schools or public libraries must reserve films through a district, system, regional or even statewide film center, meaning many libraries may be trying to reserve the same titles. Planning far in advance can help, and it is advisable to select alternatives that will fit the program plans. Ideally, films should be previewed before reserving them; in many situations this may not be possible, and librarians can be forced to rely on annotations in catalogs. By taking advantage of opportunities to see children's films and keeping notes of ways to use films seen, children's librarians can build their film knowledge.

Be willing to try something different. It is better to try a challenging film and have it flop than to limit viewers to entertaining films that will be certain hits. Library film programs should try to expand the viewing experience children have every day by offering films different from those shown on television. Look for films which take advantage of the special visual and aural qualities of the medium. Films based on children's books are also a natural for library programming. However, some great books make mediocre films and vice versa.

In selecting films for programs, choose a variety of techniques, paces, lengths, and content. Combine live-action and animated films, comedy and drama, and narrated and nonnarrated films. Use stories, documentaries, and mood, experimental, or abstract films, but don't show all documentaries or several abstract films in one program. While most children's films are now in color, some classic films in black and white are worth showing. When showing a feature-length film, include a short film at the beginning to keep latecomers from missing the beginning and to give children time to settle down. With the growth of the home video market, feature film showings in libraries may have less appeal than in the past.

Once films are selected and any other activities planned, select a catchy title for the program that conveys the theme or idea. When films arrive, librarians should try to preview them even if they have seen them before. This allows librarians to plan how to introduce the films and to be sure the

film is not damaged before showing it to a group. In cases where the film has not been seen before ordering, librarians can be sure it was what they expected and make any necessary program adjustments.

How a film is introduced affects how children see it. Sometimes, simply giving the title may be sufficient. In other cases librarians may want to set a mood or framework for viewing the film. A film set in a historic or foreign setting may need some explanation or information about the setting, culture, or events surrounding the film. Asking the children to imagine they are a different size or a particular insect or animal as they watch certain nature films can give them a different perspective. If a film doesn't have a plot, children will often respond better if they know that fact so they don't spend the viewing time trying to figure it out. In the same way, telling children about foreign phrases or that a film is in black and white frees them to concentrate on what's happening instead of being surprised at what they are seeing and hearing. Don't give a plot summary, but create a background so that children can understand and experience the film in a positive way. Doing an activity with children is another way to introduce a film. Children can pretend to be an animal featured in a film or talk about the topic of the film as either an introduction or conclusion. They can guess what it is about from the title.

Some films speak for themselves, but other films may benefit from discussion. Don't ask children if they liked the film as this will cut off discussion, and children will often say no about a strange or unusual film before they have a chance to think about it. If a film is discussed, avoid asking content questions and focus instead on extending the experience of the film. Questions about how the film made children feel, what things they observed in the film, what sounds they heard, or what the film made them think about will stimulate discussion.

Media programs are dependent on equipment, and it is important that equipment be well maintained so that problems do not occur during programs. Keeping projector film tracks and video heads clean will prevent scratches and damage to materials. Always have a spare bulb, adapter plug, extension cord, and other supplies handy, including when equipment is taken out of the library, to avoid minor problems that can cause delays or cancellations. Be sure equipment is set up in advance. Stay with it during a program to be sure nothing malfunctions. Stopping equipment quickly when problems develop can minimize damage. At the end of a film, make the showing look more professional by turning off the light and then the sound rather than just turning off the projector which can have a jarring effect. Have sufficient reels on hand to avoid rewinding films during a program.

Being a visual and aural activity, watching film can lead naturally into other activities such as art, drama, and music. These activities can also give the children a way to express their response to a film and to extend its experience. This is especially true for films which are not straightforward, live-action story films based on books. Films which use interesting techniques, or create feelings or moods, can stimulate creative activities. Sometimes a film which is difficult for children can be made more accessible and understandable through an activity. For example, a film that uses clay animation is a natural lead-in to working with clay, play dough or other molding material. After children watch several films involving food, let them create their own incredible recipes. With fairy tales, show a film and compare it to a picture book of the story, or show two different film versions of the same story and discuss them. This will give children the opportunity to see how the choice of visual images affects the mood and impact of the story. This would be effective using a live-action and an animated version of the same fairy tale. With younger children, an animated fairy tale or other story can lead into children acting out the story or pretending to be a character or object in the film. Film can also be used in conjunction with a special speaker. Showing a film about a pet can be a wonderful introduction to a pet store owner or veterinarian talking about pet selection and care. Always have a display of related books and other materials and briefly booktalk a few books during the program.

Aside from viewing films and filmstrips children will also enjoy creating these materials themselves. Some libraries have had video projects where children learn how to make videotapes and make their own films. In many school media centers this is a standard activity, and students film other students in activities, do school newscasts, and make creative films. They may do videotaped book reviews that others can use for peer comments about books. They learn how to edit and add

sound tracks. Children can also make a series of slides to tell a story. Films, filmstrips or slide programs can be made without a camera by drawing directly on blank film. Blank 16mm film leader and filmstrip film can be purchased or old film can be bleached to remove the film emulsion and make clear film. Children draw on the film with non-water-based, felt-tip markers. They can also use crayon to cover the surface and scratch in their design with pins. When using 16mm film be sure children are aware that 16mm film requires 24 frames for each second on the screen. Designs need to be repeated numerous times to make them recognizable when they are projected. Filmstrips and slides do not require repetition. Children can make their own drawn films, or a group film can be made with each child working on a section. When the film is projected, encourage children to identify their contributions. Projecting this will dirty equipment because inks may rub off in the film channel, so it needs to be cleaned afterwards. Sound tracks can be made with cassette tapes using recorded music or the children's own sounds.

FILMSTRIPS

A filmstrip and a film do not have the same effect. By its nature, a filmstrip is stiffer, and the audience is aware of each frame change. It is a series of pictures projected onto a screen with no motion in the pictures. Although filmstrips are a series of slides mounted onto a strip, filmstrips for children generally lack the creativity seen in some slide shows. They are mostly straightforward stories, retellings of books or factual information. However, they have often been widely used because they are less expensive than film and easily portable. However, with the increase in affordable videotapes, filmstrip use may decline in the future. Many filmstrips are being transferred to videotape.

In the case of filmstrips based on picture books, their chief advantage is the size of the image. In cases where book pictures are very small, it may be the only way to share the story with a group. However, books involve the listener and the reader with each other as they are read aloud, and that personal touch is lost with narrated filmstrips. When children watch filmstrips during a story program, they often act differently than when a story is being read. They watch closely, just as they watch television, but active response declines.

When using filmstrips, be sure to choose quality ones with well-done narrations and musical background. Avoid stories with poor illustrations and weak plots. If the filmstrip is based on a picture book, always have the book to show to children. Children do not necessarily connect the two, even if the book cover is shown on the filmstrip. If it is based on a fairy tale, show the children a collection with the story or a picture book version. If the filmstrip comes with a printed copy of the text, occasionally show the pictures and read the text rather than using the tape to maintain that personal connection with the children. With filmstrips based on songs, make viewing into a sing-along activity. Use filmstrips as they enhance a program, not to fill up time.

One of the best uses of filmstrips is for individual viewing by a child. An individual filmstrip viewer with headphones can be set up in a corner of the children's area or media center. Some libraries put out a selection of filmstrips each week that the children may view. Videotapes may also be used in this way.

Some public libraries also circulate films, videos, or filmstrips to day care centers and other groups, as well as to individuals, and sometimes offer a projector for loan as well. This provides materials which most child care programs would not have available otherwise. In the same way, media centers loan materials for individual classroom use.

RECORDINGS

While the primary use of recordings may be for checkout, many libraries provide a place for children to listen to records and/or cassettes in the library. Headphones allow children to listen without disturbing others. Multiple jacks make it possible for several children with headphones to listen to the same recording simultaneously. Recordings can also be used as a programming resource. Background music may introduce and end programs. Recordings with songs and music activities can be used in programs. Sometimes using a recording of an activity song can free the librarian to interact with the children instead of having to focus on the lyrics. Using storytelling or long spoken-word recordings is not recommended in programs because it is hard to keep a group's attention focused on a recording. Listening to a storyteller on record is not

the same as having one there in person. However, a recorded poem could be used effectively with slides or pictures or to stimulate a drama activity.

REALIA

Realia is best used on an individual basis by children. Provide a place for parents and children to use toys and games in the library. The library may hold parent and child classes to teach parents how to play and use toys with children. They may also have workshops for parents and other adults. Some libraries have games for older children and provide a place where games can be played. Libraries sometime sponsor tournaments based on chess, checker, or other popular board games.

COMPUTERS

The primary use of computers and software in the library will be by individuals or small groups of two or three. Because children like to use computers in small groups, that should be taken into consideration in planning a computer area. Most libraries have found computers very popular and have had to write computer-use policies and limit length of access in order to meet demand.

The computer can also be used to enhance library activities. Children can input reviews or comments about books they read which can be used by other children. They can be encouraged to write poetry or stories on it and display them in the library. A library can sponsor an exhibit of computer graphics or hold a contest of stories or poetry written using word processing. The library can also sponsor programs for children or parents about computers and selecting appropriate software. Either public libraries or media centers could also sponsor a computer club for children where they can exchange information and learn more about computers. By incorporating computers into library activities for children and families, the library promotes itself as an agency interested in the new technology and has the potential of reaching children who are not regular library users.

By making computers available to children, libraries and media centers also provide opportunities for children who do not have computers at home. Some people feel that the new technology will further separate the "haves" and the "have nots" in society, and the library can play a role in equalizing access, just as it does with print materials.

BIBLIOGRAPHY

Association for Library Service to Children. *Programming to Help Children Use Media Creatively.* Program Support Publications # 9. Chicago: American Library Association, 1983.

Baker, D. Philip. *School and Public Library Media Programs for Children and Young Adults.* Syracuse, NY: Gaylord Professional Publications, 1977.

Center for Understanding Media. *Doing the Media.* Rev. ed. New York: McGraw-Hill, 1978.
    Presents activities, ideas, and resources.

Emens, Carol A. "Copyright Considerations." *School Library Journal* 32 (Feb 1986): 35.

Gaffney, Maureen. *More Films Kids Like.* Chicago: American Library Association, 1977.

Gaffney, Maureen and Gerry Bond Laybourne. *What to Do When the Lights Go On: A Comprehensive Guide to 16mm Films and Related Activities for Children.* Phoenix, AZ: Oryx Press, 1981.

Gothberg. Helen M. *Television and Video in Libraries and Schools.* Hamden, CT: Library Professional Publications, 1983.

Hunt, Mary Alice, ed. *A Multimedia Approach to Children's Literature.* 3rd ed. Chicago: American Library Association, 1983.

Lacey, Richard A. *Seeing with Feeling: Film in the Classroom.* Philadelphia, PA: Saunders, 1972.
    Offers techniques for introducing and discussing films.

Mathias, Linda. "The Cable Connection...Our Experience with Cable TV." *Illinois Libraries* 67 (Jan 1985): 44-48.

Ward-Callaghan, Linda. "The Effect of Emerging Technologies on Children's Library Service." *Library Trends* 35 (Winter 1987): 437-447.

Summer Reading and Other Programs to Encourage Reading

Incentive programs have been widely used in libraries to encourage children to read. Generally, they last for a limited time period and use a theme as well as awards, prizes or other recognition. Summer reading programs have been a tradition in many public libraries, but they are certainly not the only way to approach summer services for children. In schools, a reading program may be held anytime during the school year.

Behind all reading programs is the idea that children will read more when there is some incentive. However, reading programs are not universally applauded. Some librarians feel that they take time in planning and record keeping that could better be used for other activities. Others feel they bring out competitiveness and emphasize how many books are read rather than what the children are reading. Programs which require a certain number of books to be read or which award prizes or special recognition for reading a large number of books aren't really going to encourage the slow or poor readers who know they can't compete with the better readers. The very process of awarding prizes for reading a certain number of books, no matter how small, may give the idea that reading is not fun in itself, but something one is "paid" to do. If reading drops way off when a program has ended, this may indicate children were reading for the awards alone.

Summer and other reading programs have some good points. An appealing theme and planned program can help attract children and parents to the library. Particularly in a public library setting, parents who might not bring children just to check out books may bring them if they are signed up in a reading program. If librarians use the reading programs as a way to talk more with children about what they are reading, it can give them an opportunity to get to know the children and their reading tastes better. Providing an incentive to read may help some children learn that reading is enjoyable in itself. For some children the external reward and recognition may be effective in overcoming reluctance to read beyond required books. Other library programs such as film programs, puppet shows, storytelling, or lessons in library use may not draw children to the book collection. This is one library activity that focuses on books and reading. By offering children an incentive to read and getting them to read more, it gives them practice in reading skills and helps them improve their reading. Since summer is a time when many children lose some of their newly acquired skills, a program which encourages reading can help retain and improve skills.

In *Summer Learning and the Effects of Schooling* (1978), Barbara Heyns describes her research on summer reading and provides justification for some type of summer reading encouragement in libraries. Heyns found that the number of books read during a summer is consistently related to achievement gains. Reading is the single summer activity most strongly and consistently related to summer learning. It increases children's vocabulary scores. In fact, the use of the public library is more predictive of vocabulary gains than attending summer school. Heyns found that children in every income group who read six or more books over the summer gained more in reading achievement than children who did not. The largest gain among Black children tended to be among the more affluent, although children at every income level but the very lowest gained two or more months of achievement over those children who read less.

Heyns also found that the major factors determining whether children read over the summer were use of the public library, sex (girls tended to read more than boys, but they also watched more television), socioeconomic status, and distance from home to library. The farther children lived from library service, the less likely they were to use it. More than any other public agency, the public library contributed to the subjects' intellectual growth over the summer. Unlike summer school programs, which attract a small percentage of children, the library was used regularly by over one half of the children in her sample and attracted children from diverse backgrounds.

Analyzing the library's activities and considering the positive and negative aspects of reading programs will help librarians decide whether reading programs are right for their libraries. Just because there has always been one is not in itself justification for its continuation.

For public libraries, help with summer reading materials is available from a variety of sources. In an attempt to improve the quality of materials and help individual libraries with planning, over 20 states now have statewide summer reading programs available, coordinated mostly by state libraries but in some cases by library organizations. These provide materials to libraries on a theme. Depending on the state, the cost may be paid for by the state library, or the materials may be sold to the libraries at cost. In a few situations, camera-ready copy is provided, and libraries produce the materials themselves. Materials available usually include posters, bookmarks, folders or sheets for children to record books read, and certificates. They may include other small incentives for libraries to use as they choose. Manuals assembled by staff or committees provide ideas for running the program and bibliographies, suggestions for programs, games, puzzles, and other activities related to the theme. Participation is optional, but libraries may find the cooperative effort a time-saver since designing a program from scratch can be very time consuming.

The American Library Association has also made materials available for use in summer reading programs. Commercial reading program materials can also be purchased for summer or other reading programs. While use of any of these materials does remove some freedom in designing a program, the savings in planning time allows librarians to spend time planning activities rather than program materials. They are probably most beneficial for small and medium-sized library systems and independent libraries where limited staff and resources often make it difficult to plan and produce a quality program and materials. With either commercial or state program materials, libraries are free to determine their own program structure, although a program should be the same throughout a library system to facilitate publicity and avoid confusion for patrons who use more than one library outlet.

A good reading program requires good planning. Even though it may be a traditional activity done every year, librarians should rethink goals and objectives. Consider why the library is doing this and be sure the program fits in with the overall goals for library service to the children. What does the library staff want to see happen because of the reading program both for the library and for the children who participate? What children does the library hope to reach with the program? Decide on the age range to be included. Consider if there is a target group the library wants to make special efforts to get involved in the program. For example, the library may want to work to get more children from a nearby housing project involved. It may need to reach more children who live far from the library and need extra incentives. It may want to plan modifications and special publicity to encourage mentally retarded, deaf, blind, and other disabled children to participate in the program. With a greater number of school-aged children in organized programs for the summer, consider also what accommodations the library could make so that groups coming to the library can participate or so that children can participate at a day care or other site.

A typical overall goal for summer reading programs is to encourage children to read as a way to help them learn to enjoy books and reading. Other goals include helping children to develop reading skills and to become comfortable using the library. Some objectives might be to increase participation over previous programs by a certain percent or number, to have a certain number of programs or activities in conjunction with the reading program, and to prepare a certain number of booklists to increase interest in reading. Specific, measurable objectives will help in program evaluation.

Once goals and objectives are established, staff can design a program to meet them. The budget for the program should be submitted as part of the annual budget request and should include the cost of printed materials needed for the program and expenses for related programs including supplies, film rentals, or speaker or performer fees. The projected cost of supplies for special displays, exhibits, publicity and even refreshments should be included.

Examine the program from previous years if the library has had one and decide if the procedures, rules, and regulations worked well. Consider if they encouraged or hindered children's participation. Common barriers are short registration periods and excessive requirements. Keep focused on the idea that the library wants the program to encourage reading. Avoid restrictions and requirements that will work against this goal.

Programs often require children to read a certain number of books to earn a certificate or prize. Requiring too large a number of books discourages slower readers and encourages reading below skill and interest level just to fulfill requirements. It can also lead to cheating. Anyone who has run this type of program knows children check out a big stack of easy books in order to complete the program or list books they haven't read. At the same time, requiring children to read on their level will discourage children who are poor readers from participating.

Librarians may want to consider an alternative approach to structuring the program. Some libraries use a contract system. Children decide how many books they think they can read and sign a contract or agreement to read that number. This is a much less competitive approach, but librarians must be able to talk with children and help them make realistic estimates. Some children may want to contract for only one or two books; other children think very ambitiously and want to set unrealistic goals for themselves. The emphasis here is on individual achievement. Other libraries have kept track of visits to the library rather than books read, working on the assumption that children will borrow books if they visit the library regularly.

Another approach is to give children a sticker or some small incentive for every book or for every certain number of books read. Another is to stress the total number of books read by children in the program rather than the number read by each child. A figure relating to the theme can be hung in the children's area and children add a part to it for each book read. For example, children could add parts of an animal's tail for each book read and work together to get it as long as possible. Some libraries set no requirements, letting children record books read for their own pleasure and creating a club feeling through a weekly newsletter, activity and game sheet, and special activities.

It is not a good idea to award prizes to the child who reads the most books. This emphasizes quantity over quality, and children who are not eager readers will lose interest quickly since they know they will not win a prize. Reading programs should encourage a love of reading, not a desire to read the most or to be the best reader. Often parents or teachers will want recognition for the children who read the most, and librarians need to feel comfortable discussing why this is not done.

Another decision to be made is the age range for participation. It is not really necessary to have an upper age limit because children will stop participating on their own by age 10 or 11, and if an older child wants to join the program, it doesn't really matter. A program in a school may choose to focus on one or two grades at a time.

It is necessary to decide if public library programs will be for children who can read or whether they will have a read-to-me component for preschool children. Traditionally summer reading programs were for reading children, but in recent years many libraries have included preschoolers or run a separate parallel program for them. This has largely developed from parent requests because younger brothers and sisters feel left out. In a read-to-me program, a parent or other adult reads to the child and the family keeps track of books read. While it is good to be able to have all children included, having a read-to-me component does remove the excitement of being old enough to join the program when a child finishes kindergarten or first grade. It also may make children tire of the program at a younger age. An alternative approach is to have a special preschool reading program at another time of the year.

If the library is not using materials from some other source, staff will need to select a theme and design needed materials with lots of child appeal. Often themes related to a popular topic work well.

The theme should appeal to both girls and boys and to the older children, since they will not participate in anything that sounds like it is for younger children. It should also have potential for developing programs and other activites that relate to it.

Once the basic design of the program is decided the library can plan the organizational details. Summer reading programs usually last from six to ten weeks. Programs in schools can run for whatever length of time seems appropriate, but it should be limited or children will lose interest. Remember that the length of time children can read for the program does not have to match the time in which special activities are offered. A library may do programs for children for six weeks during the summer, but children may read for the program all summer long.

Don't plan the program in isolation. For a summer program be aware of the dates public and private schools end and begin, vacation Bible school dates, local swimming pool hours, and other regular community and special events. In a school avoid planning the program at the same time there is a big sports or other promotion. While all conflicts can't be avoided, they can be minimized. When dates are selected let others know so they will not plan conflicting activities. This is especially important in smaller communities where the pool of children is small.

If the library registers children for the program, keep information to a minimum. The less paperwork involved, the more time staff have to work with children. At the least most libraries want children to register to give the library a record of participation. If the program uses reading records, it is much less paperwork if children keep track of these themselves. If children take records home, the library will have to replace a few lost ones, but this is a minimal expense.

Many libraries award certificates to children and plan special programs or parties to end the program on a festive note. If the library distributes certificates at a final celebration, invite a special guest such as a local official to distribute the certificates. Plan a way to distribute certificates to children who do not come to a party.

Other libraries distribute certificates to children in the fall through the schools. To do this, the library should contact the schools for approval in the spring, then arrange to distribute the certificates through the librarian or classroom teachers. It is

necessary to know what school and grade the child will attend in the fall.

Another approach is to give certificates to children as they complete the program. This solves the problem of certificates that are not claimed at summer's end, but it can make children feel that once they have finished the program they have finished reading for the summer. If this approach is used, staff should tell the children as they give them a certificate that they hope the children will keep reading and visiting the library. School programs have fewer problems with distributing certificates or awards because the children are there every day. Some libraries have eliminated certificates as time-consuming paperwork and have found that they are not missed.

Many libraries also give children some other small token for completing the program. In recent years food coupons from fast food restaurants have been popular choices. In accepting a coupon or pass from a business, remember their purpose is to increase business. Don't save something for a prize such as a button or bumper sticker which would be much more effective used as a promotional item early in the program.

Libraries may also want to consider not limiting the materials used for the reading program to books. Perhaps a child could include tapes or records to which they listened. This would make the program more accessible to the learning disabled and other children with reading difficulties. Allow blind children to participate and read talking books from their Library for the Blind. Allow children to include craft and informational books that they may use without reading them in their entirety.

Keep statistics about the program for evaluation and justification for future budget requests and planning. Statistics kept by library outlet show where response is better or less than average. Keep records of the number of children enrolled by age or grade, the number receiving certificates or completing requirements, the total number of books read, the number who registered but never participated, the number who attend related programs, and the number of children who received library cards in order to join. Schools would want to keep statistics by class. Note the quantity of materials left over to help in planning for the future. Calculate the total costs for the program, and compare statistics with previous programs to determine if participation increased or decreased. Calculate the percentage of children in the community participating. Analyze use by library outlets to determine if it was less successful in certain areas. Determine what age range participated the most. Let these statistics offer some direction for planning future programs. Let children help evaluate the program through a questionnaire or interviews and note their responses.

Good publicity and promotion are essential to a successful reading program. People must know about it to participate. Publicity should be heavier as the program begins but should continue throughout the program. Public libraries need to explain the program to all staff. Summer reading often seems more of a headache than anything to the staff member who sees it only in terms of masses of children and more books to handle. Those in daily contact with patrons can build interest by telling children and parents about the program but will do so only if the children's department has generated enthusiasm for the program.

Schools need to get the teachers behind a reading program and let parents know about it through a school newsletter or flyer. Public library programs also need to publicize in schools. Many libraries send staff to visit classes or assemblies to talk about the program. School administrators and staff can be helpful in promoting it if they see how it will benefit their students. One library persuaded a school district to include flyers about summer reading at the public library in final report cards, and participation increased significantly. Newspaper, radio, and television are also important vehicles for publicizing the program.

Reading incentive programs can provide an excellent opportunity for school and public libraries to work together to encourage children's reading. Some schools loan public libraries extra copies of popular titles to help meet demands. In communities where school libraries open during the summer for children to use, they could be involved in the same program. If school libraries acted as cosponsors, children could register for the program and begin reading during the last weeks of school.

Reading programs offered during the school year could be cooperatively sponsored as well. Even in public libraries reading programs do not have to be confined to the summer. Another time of year may be preferable for a preschool reading program. A reading program for school children during the school year should be shorter in duration and with few requirements since children are busier.

School and public libraries could also work together on a family reading program. For this, the entire family signs up to read either together or separately for so many minutes a day. They receive a certificate for keeping the commitment for a specified time period. This type of program is designed to help families develop a habit of making time in their schedules for regular reading.

Another way to approach reading aloud programs with preschoolers is to have a special one for children who come to story hour or in cooperation with child development programs that use the library. In the latter situation, center staff could introduce the program to parents and encourage them to join and to use the library. The library and child development center could give a joint certificate. This could be an excellent way to reach these children's parents who may not use the library or read to their children.

Reading programs have often become stale and uninteresting because they have been done year in and year out with little changes. However, they do not need to be that way. When well planned and thought out they can be an effective way to stimulate children's reading and make them feel reading is both important and fun.

Bibliography

Association for Library Service to Children. *Programming for Summer.* Program Support Publications #5. Chicago: American Library Association, 1982.

Evaluating Summer Reading Programs. Youth Services Division, Pennsylvania Library Association and State Library of Pennsylvania. Unpublished LSCA (Library Services and Construction Act) manuscript, 1986.

Heyns, Barbara. *Summer Learning and the Effects of Schooling.* San Diego, CA: Academic Press, 1978

Somerville, Mary. "How to Knock the Stuffings Out of Your Summer Reading Program." *Top of the News* 37 (Spring 1981): 265-274.

Young, Diana. "Reading for the Fun of It: Summer Reading Programs." *Public Libraries* 18, no. 2 (Summer 1979): 38-41.

Other Activities and Programs

While previous chapters discussed various types and techniques of library programming, many programs and activities do not fit strictly into a single mold. Programs often incorporate a variety of techniques, such as combining storytelling, poetry, and film along with music and art activities. Many programs include a variety of activities all having a common theme. In addition to specific techniques previously discussed, libraries can incorporate music, arts and crafts, choral reading, puzzles and games into programming. Libraries also do special exhibits and displays, sponsor photography or writing contests or exhibits, hold tournaments, and a variety of other activities in and out of the library in order to promote the library. They sponsor book discussion groups and do booktalks in schools and to other groups of children. Programs and activities are limited only by imagination and creativity and the need to relate activities in some way to the library.

Numerous books are available to provide program ideas for both school and public libraries. Two good examples are *This Way to Books* (1983) and *Celebrations* (1985) by Caroline Feller Bauer, which are excellent sources of creative program ideas. Each idea is clearly described and lists all materials and resources needed for the program.

Stories, poems, films, music, art and crafts, puppet productions, and other activities on a theme can be pulled together to create programs that allow children to explore an idea, place, or time through a combination of activities. Programs can focus on various countries or cultural groups, seasons and other phenomena of nature, or almost any topic. A program could feature a Japanese folk tale, a film or puppet show set in Japan, and a simple origami activity. Favorite or well-known books or authors can establish a theme for a program. Laura Ingalls Wilder's "Little House" books could be used as a basis for a festival on pioneer days, including demonstrations of old crafts, exhibits of typical household items, a nineteenth-century game, storytelling, and a craft activity. Other books such as *Alice in Wonderland* and *Winnie the Pooh* offer lots of programming possibilities. Try programs which focus on the nonsense of Dr. Seuss or the tales of Hans Christian Andersen. One can also use a genre of stories such as fairy tales, mysteries, or nonsense as a basis for programming.

SPEAKERS AND PERFORMERS

Guest speakers or performers provide variety in programming. Many good programs can be done by local people who are willing to talk about their work, hobby, or interest for either a modest fee or no cost. Libraries should try to put money in the budget for fees and honorariums. Be grateful for volunteers, but don't expect local authors, celebrities, and experts to always donate their time. A speaker or performer may be combined with a related film or story to give another dimension or viewpoint to the subject. In the program on Japan mentioned earlier, a local person of Japanese descent or one who has visited there could bring some arts, crafts, or traditional clothing to show as part of a larger program. On other occasions the speaker or performer may be sufficient for a complete program. Always do a related book display and, whenever possible, a short booklist to accompany a speaker and direct children to library materials.

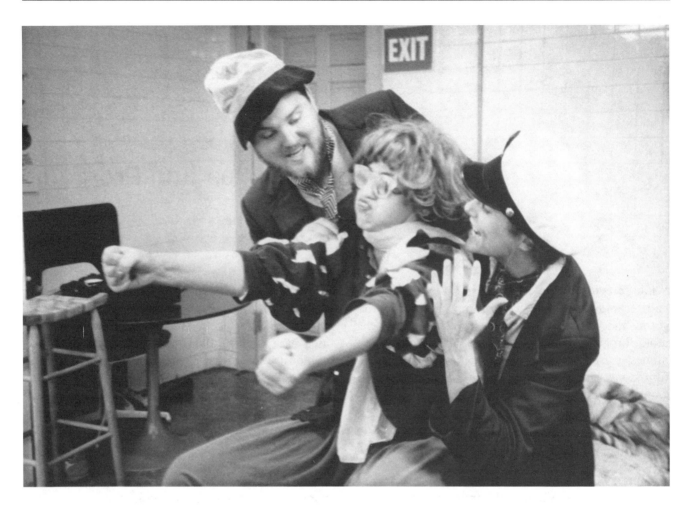

FIGURE 8. Professional theater groups can bring drama to children in the library. (Chopstick Theater, Charleston, SC) (This photograph is from a production of *The Adventures of Mr. Toad*, based on Kenneth Grahame's *The Wind and the Willows*.)

Keeping a list of potential speakers makes it easier to find speakers when you need them. Librarians can develop a file of possible resource people through newspaper articles, staff and patron recommendations, clubs and organizations, word of mouth, schools, and other librarians. When the newspaper runs a feature on someone who just spent a year in Greece, add the name to the file. A file of this sort would be an excellent resource for school and public librarians to build together. It would be useful not only for themselves but for answering queries from teachers and patrons.

Among the resource people who could be useful to know about are police officers; firefighters; drivers of emergency vehicles, tractor trailers, or construction vehicles; bicyclists or a bicycle shop owner; computer experts; a veterinarian; a pet shop owner or local animal breeder or judge; stamp, coin and other collectors; hobbyists with interests such as model railroading, bird-watching, or star-gazing;

craftspeople and artists; people who come from another country or who travel extensively; local folk dance groups or dance students; sports heroes; and almost anyone else who enjoys sharing a special interest, talent, or hobby. Teenagers and children may enjoy sharing their interest with other children. Zoos, museums, orchestras and bands, and other community groups can also be good sources of programs. Many of these people can also be resources for materials for special displays and exhibits.

Professional storytellers, puppeteers, magicians, and actors are among those who may be available for special programs either as part of a tour or through arrangements for a special visit. While many public libraries have money for special events in library budgets, many others do not, particularly those in smaller communities. Although fees may seem high to librarians used to programming on a tight budget, most of these people are trying to make a living or at least meet expenses for a part-time avocation. It is important to recognize the training and effort that goes into their work. Before deciding some special event for the library is too expensive, explore various possibilities for paying for it. The worst that can happen from exploring other resources is that the needed funds won't materialize. Often, Friends of the Library groups or parent-teacher organizations may be willing to help sponsor a special performance. Small arts or humanities grants may be available from state or local arts and humanities organizations. Other community groups or businesses may be willing to be sponsors. School districts and public libraries may be able to pool resources to bring in an individual or group for several performances in both of their facilities.

Authors provide another resource for programs, but don't expect them to volunteer their time. Speaking to groups is an opportunity to talk about their writing but it is also time away from writing. Unless librarians know authors personally, most prefer to be contacted through their publishers. This is a good activity for schools and public libraries to plan together to cut expenses, especially if the author has to travel. An author could talk at school and then do a reading or talk to parents or take some other approach at a public library program. Schools in particular have done some imaginative programs with authors. A popular program has been doing telephone interviews with a special receiver so that a group of children can listen to and question the author.

BOOK DISCUSSION GROUPS

Book discussion groups can be very enjoyable and can help children develop critical skills and broaden their reading base. A book discussion group needs to be offered for a specific age group. In a school setting it may be done for a single grade level or as an enrichment activity for selected students. Programs can be highly structured or quite informal. Junior Great Books is an established book discussion program which uses specified books, largely classics, and a set format and discussion questions. It is sponsored by the Great Books Foundation, 307 North Michigan Avenue, Chicago, Illinois 60601. While its structure and stress on classics may be too limiting for many librarians, its training program is highly regarded.

Librarians can also set up their own program. Children can all read the same book, or read different books on a common theme. They may also meet to share informally whatever they have been reading. To be successful a book discussion group must have set meeting times. By creating a feeling of a club, the children will develop a feeling of group unity. Choose a clever title rather than calling it a book discussion group. Two that have been used are "The Book Bunch" and "R.A.T.S." (The Reading and Talking Society). A similar group could be formed to critically view and discuss films.

Another small-group program is a creative writing seminar lasting several sessions and led by a local writer or creative writing teacher. Children could write their own poems or stories and learn how to make a book.

BOOKTALKS

At most programs, librarians can find a few minutes to include brief booktalks about some books related to the program theme. This is an excellent way to be sure that children are encouraged to read as part of every program.

Longer, more formal booktalks are a wonderful way to encourage children to read. The idea behind booktalking is to pique interest by telling enough about the book to capture interest without revealing the entire plot. Generally, the librarian gives a little background about the story and chooses one or two incidents to convey the flavor of the book. Booktalks can be included when school and other groups visit the public library, or when classes go to the library media center, and they can be shared with children in classrooms by both school and public librarians. Often public librarians visit schools to do booktalks and promote use of the library. School media specialists may give booktalks to classes as well, possibly tailoring them to topics or projects being studied at that time. A good booktalk on fiction about the Civil War provides students with ideas for books to help understand the war from a human point of view. A booktalk may be quite informal, sharing titles and brief descriptions, or it may be more formal, where a carefully prepared presentation about several books may take 15 or more minutes.

There is really no limit to the variety of programs and activities libraries can do, depending on time and size of staff. Volunteers can be used effectively in programming to provide additional personnel. However, be sure all programs and activities are justified in terms of the library's purposes and goals and objectives. Few libraries can do everything they would like. Librarians need to make decisions on what is practical and purposeful for their situation and to be willing to try new ideas and approaches to bring children into the library.

OTHER ACTIVITIES

A children's volunteer or library aide program can attract children who like to help, and it provides them with an opportunity to learn more about libraries. It is widely used in school libraries and less often in public libraries. Children agree to volunteer at the library at certain times. In public libraries, they can learn how to shelve books, count and fold flyers, and make materials such as flannelboard figures and name tags. In schools they may also be able to check out materials and do other circulation tasks. This could be a good activity for public libraries to use with children who come regularly after school to wait for parents.

Contests and exhibitions are not programs, but they are appropriate ways to attract interest in the library and reward creative efforts. Keep any prizes modest and related to the contest and the library's purposes so that the focus remains on the product and not the prize. A poetry or story writing contest can be general or tied into a theme or holiday. For example, a Halloween story contest is a natural for children who like scary tales. In smaller communities the newspaper may be interested in printing the winning entries or a local radio station may let the winner read the story on the air. Have a bookmark contest and print the winning entries for library use. Any art or craft activity, such as photography or paper box art, can be used for a contest and exhibit. Local school art departments and other art classes for children may be willing to provide student projects for exhibitions.

Noncompetitive shows for young children can award prizes for all entries. A stuffed pet or doll show is always popular. Live pet shows are, too, but they should be outdoors if at all possible to avoid accidents. Set clear ground rules on size of pets and be prepared to deal with a pet who becomes unruly or overly excited by having some person skilled with animals present. For any contest or exhibit, do a related display highlighting "how to" books and other books related to the subject.

Still other programs can focus on self-help skills for children. Some libraries have offered programs on child safety and home skills needed by "latchkey" children, who are home alone after school. For older children, a baby-sitting clinic can be a popular and useful program and gives the library a chance to suggest baby-sitters take books to share with their charges.

In doing programs which are not directly related to the library's ordinary services, be sure to plan a way to bring related library services into the program and avoid offering programs being done by other community agencies. For example, craft programs have become popular in many libraries, but they should be linked in some way to library materials and services. Too often children come to activity programs and leave without ever giving the rest of the library more than a glance.

Participation in community festivals, fairs, and special events can be very effective ways to draw attention to the library's services for children. Participation in a parade or providing storytelling or a puppet show at a festival can attract people who don't use the public library or who are unaware of how the school libraries help their children. It also makes a positive contribution to a community event. Have an arts event for children during an adult arts festival. A booth at the county fair may attract people who never come into libraries. Remember that at wandering events such as fairs, people will not stop at one place for long, so choose short, uncomplicated stories or puppet skits rather than longer ones. Involve staff from different public and school libraries. Special events at shopping centers or malls that feature different community organizations and services for children and families are opportunities to promote libraries as well.

BIBLIOGRAPHY

Association for Library Service to Children. *Programming for Children's Book Discussion Groups.* Program Support Publications #4. Chicago: American Library Association, 1981.

———. *Programming for Multicultural Experiences.* Program Support Publications #7. Chicago: American Library Association, 1982.

Bauer, Caroline Feller. *Celebrations; Read-Aloud Holiday and Theme Programs.* New York: H. W. Wilson, 1985.

———. *This Way to Books.* New York: H. W. Wilson, 1983.

Bodart, Joni. *Book Talk!: Booktalking and School Visiting for Young Adult Audiences.* New York: H. W. Wilson, 1980.

———. *Booktalk! 2: Booktalking for All Ages and Audiences.* New York: H. W. Wilson, 1985.

———. *Booktalking with Joni Bodart.* New York: H. W. Wilson, 1986 (videotape).

Cleaver, Betty P., Barbara Chatton, and Shirley V. Morrison. *Creating Connections: Books, Kits, and Games for Children.* New York: Garland, 1986.

Haglund, Elaine J. and Marcia L. Harris. *On This Day: A Collection of Everyday Events and Activities for the Media Center, Library, and Classroom.* Littleton, CO: Libraries Unlimited, 1983.

Kobrin, Beverly. *Eyeopeners: How to Choose and Use Children's Books about Real People, Places, and Things.* New York: Viking, 1988.

Kruise, Carol Sue. *Those Bloomin' Books. A Handbook for Extending Thinking Skills.* Littleton, CO: Libraries Unlimited, 1987.

Liebold, Louise Condak. *Fireworks, Brass Bands, and Elephants: Promotional Events with Flair for Libraries and Other Nonprofit Organizations.* Phoenix, AZ: Oryx Press, 1986.

Mallett, Jerry J. and Marion Bartch. *Elementary School Library Resources Kit.* West Nyack, NY: Center for Applied Research in Education, 1984.

Marshall, Karen K. *Back to Books: 200 Library Games to Encourage Reading.* Jefferson, NC: McFarland, 1983.

Polkingham, Anne T. and Catherine Toohey. *Creative Encounters: Activities to Expand Children's Responses to Literature.* Littleton, CO: Libraries Unlimited, 1983.

Rochman, Hazel. *Tales of Love and Terror: Booktalking the Classics, Old and New.* Chicago: American Library Association, 1987.

Scales, Pat. *Dial an Author: How to Develop a Successful Reader-Writer Interview Program.* New York: Bantam, 1981.

Spirt, Diana L. *Introducing Books.* New York: Bowker, 1970.

———. *Introducing More Books.* New York: Bowker, 1978.

———. *Introducing Bookplots 3; A Book Talk Guide for Use with Readers Ages 8-12.* New York: Bowker, 1988.

Thomas, Carol H. *Merlin's Magic: A Reading Activities Idea Book for Use with Children.* Phoenix, AZ: Oryx Press, 1984.

Services to Parents and Other Adults

Services to parents and other adults working with children are an integral part of good library services to children in both school and public library settings. Influencing the adults who have continuing and important influence on children may be the most effective way over the long term to increase children's interest in reading. All libraries serving children have a responsibility to make children's families aware of the importance of children's reading and the rich resources available from the library. Public libraries should also be working to assist teachers, particularly those in early childhood education, family day care providers, and other professionals in understanding the value of books for both curriculum enrichment and children's personal growth and enjoyment. In school library media centers, working with teachers in providing resources to support classroom activities and helping them to use both fiction and nonfiction books and other materials to enhance learning is an integral part of the library media specialists' responsibilities.

Reaching out to parents is especially important because parents are children's first and most important teachers. No library can ever do enough story hours to reach every child, and a weekly story hour is not enough contact with books anyway. Lifelong positive attitudes about books and reading are most often fostered by parents and other family who read to children and enjoy reading themselves. Seeing parents read makes children want to read because they like to imitate their parents. That is why there is a greater likelihood that children of parents who cannot read or who don't read will also not be readers.

In the same way, if parents don't feel libraries are important or feel uncomfortable there, their children probably will not see the library as an enjoyable and important place. Children are often dependent on parents to bring them to the public library for individual use, and parents who don't see its value are less likely to bring them. They may also be less likely to encourage them to check out school library materials and to read beyond what is required for school. It is clear to most teachers which children come from homes where reading is valued. While teachers of young children can also be influential in establishing attitudes and values, they do not have the same influence as parents.

All parents want the best for their children and want their children to do well in school. Their concern that children be ready for school has led to an ever-increasing interest in pushing young children to learn academic skills. There has been a proliferation of books on the subject and more and more toys promise to teach children specific skills. More preschool programs emphasize academic skills usually learned in primary school even though specialists in early childhood development believe this may in the long run be detrimental to learning.

Early learning of reading skills will not turn children into eager readers and learners if the desire to learn is not developed. Research shows that reading aloud to children is still the best predictor of reading success in school. This is the message that librarians need to talk about again and again. When possible, both parents should be involved in reading to children. It is important for fathers to give their sons the role model that men read too.

In contemporary society families come in all different shapes and sizes with varying social and economic problems, family configurations, opportunities, and experiences. No one method of outreach to parents is sufficient to reach all families. In planning public library services to parents, working with adult services staff will result in a coordinated plan. This is an excellent area as well for school library media specialists and public librarians to work together because they have a common goal of wanting to make families aware of their role in their children's reading development.

Services to parents can take a variety of approaches. Libraries may concentrate on increasing book awareness of parents or they may try to offer programs and other activities on the wider topic of child growth and development. They may try to help parents who are already interested in their children's reading to know more about children's literature. They may work to increase awareness of the library as a community resource. If efforts are to be successful, work with parents must be a continuing effort and not a single program or booklist. A coordinated plan would involve using all methods possible to reach parents.

To reach successfully those parents who are not library users takes a commitment and a willingness to get out of the library and to go to where parents are as well as offering activities and aids in the library. Reaching parents often requires innovative and time-consuming approaches. As useful as they are, brochures and parent programs in libraries will not reach people who never use libraries. This is not to say that programs in libraries are not worthwhile, but limiting efforts to in-library activity may mean librarians are largely preaching to the converted. Consider ways to reach people outside the library walls.

A program or series of programs on reading to children and children's books can be offered in a library from time to time. Although response is not large, even reaching a few parents can make this program worthwhile. Some libraries have also had successful discussion groups for parents to read and talk about children's books, which helps parents learn more about what their children are reading and the variety of books available for children. If staffing allows, programs on children's books and reading could be offered during story times or other

programs, or a special story time could be held during the parent program to solve baby-sitting problems. Cassette tapes and videotapes on reading to children can be purchased for circulation to parents and groups.

Getting out of the library and talking to community groups about reading to children can be more effective. Develop a short, snappy presentation on why reading is important and what parents can do. Give it a title that relates reading to children to success in school and life because this will help stimulate interest. Don't wait for invitations to speak. Contact community groups and organizations and ask to do a program for them. Think about groups such as parent-teacher organizations; child development center parent groups; Junior Women's Clubs, Lions, Jaycees, Rotary, and other service clubs; organizations of parents of disabled children; single parents; and other special needs groups. Churches often have special series of programs for parents. When you see information about some agency or group offering parenting classes or seminars, volunteer to do a presentation on reading.

Aside from a lack of time, probably the thing that keeps many librarians from doing this is fear of talking to a group. Like most activities, it becomes easier each time it is done. By developing a standard presentation, which can be adapted to individual groups, librarians can become comfortable with a presentation. A speech should include a brief introduction to the library and why it is concerned with children's reading. It should discuss why parents should read to children, ways adults can help children through reading, suggestions about what books are appropriate for different ages, some hints on how to read aloud, and the value of daily reading. Let people know what the library offers for children in terms of the variety of materials, programs, and activities, and staff who can help. Always take some favorite books to use as examples, including one or two related to specific interests of the group. In a presentation to a group of men, include some children's books on fishing or sports. At a church group, show some of the library's Bible stories. A short videotape or slide presentation about the library or reading to children can be a great help as well. Take brochures about the library, children's reading, and booklists to distribute.

Booklists are also valuable for parents who often wonder what they should read to their children. Lists of recommended books for various age groups can be distributed in the library and at places such as health clinics, doctors' offices, child development centers, and social service agencies. Make booklists attractive and inviting with a goal of creating interest rather than being comprehensive. Too many titles can overwhelm people. Lists dealing with special needs such as going to the hospital, divorce, or a new baby are useful. Local bookstores may be interested in cooperating on a list of books for holiday giving. Basic information about reading to children and a booklist prepared by the library could be included in packets of information given to new parents in the hospital.

Most libraries have many useful bibliographies and books about children's reading that parents and other adults don't know about. Booklists about books in the adult collection on child development, making toys, cooking for children and other topics can make people aware that the library has these materials. A parents' corner or shelf in the children's area is a good way to make parents and other adults aware of these resources. Books related to children's reading can be placed here permanently along with periodicals such as *Horn Book, Parent's Choice* and others that provide ideas for parents and teachers. Rather than duplicating other books relating to parenting and child growth and development, books can be borrowed from the general collection each month for a display. Feature topics such as child development, nutrition, toys to make and buy, or finding child care.

Don't limit promotion of children's reading to the children's area of the library. A display in the adult area will be seen by those who do not come into the children's area. Use special weeks such as the Week of the Young Child (April), National Library Week (April), or Children's Book Week (November) to focus adult attention on children's reading. Photographs of parents reading to children displayed with comments from the parents about what they enjoy most about reading to their children make a strong statement. Ask children of a variety of ages to tell you the title of their favorite book and why. Use their comments and the books for a display. Quotations from famous people or community leaders about the importance of reading can also be the basis for an exhibit. Ask the superintendent of schools, a government official, a minister, a teacher, and a business person to write a brief statement about why reading is important in their lives. An exhibit of books suggested for gift giving or of the Notable Children's Books of the year placed in the adult area can raise awareness of children's books and reading. At library programs for adults, include a few children's books on the program topic in the book display.

Try getting parents and other adults into the library by hosting workshops or programs on other topics relating to children such as choosing child care, talking to children about sex, helping children deal with death, or preparing your child to start school. Use resource people from your area to talk or to lead a discussion based on a film or videotape. Always include a display of children's and adult books related to the topic. Try to do occasional displays in other community agencies such as social service and health agencies where people are likely to be who do not use the library.

Make use of newspapers, radio, and television to talk about reading to children. The media will generally be more interested if a request for an interview is tied to a special event or promotion.

Schools have special opportunities to reach parents. Library media specialists can do displays related to topics of parent-teacher association meetings. They can make good use of parent nights by planning a special activity in the library media center. If the school has a newsletter, they can include something about new books and the media center and what it is doing.

Media specialists, children's librarians, and others interested in children's reading can join together to promote reading through a special promotion using techniques such as bumper stickers, billboards, brochures, and other promotional items. By forming a coalition for promoting reading among schools, public libraries, teacher organizations, and concerned parents, more can be accomplished than when a single organization tries to do it all. Libraries have persuaded supermarkets to print and use a library-oriented message on grocery sacks for a designated time period. Messages about reading have appeared on milk cartons, city buses, and store marquees. Librarians never know what may be possible in this area until they ask. Fast-food franchises occasionally will use a special tray liner to promote a community service. One national fast-food franchise claims more people come to their restaurants each week than read newspapers, so these unorthodox approaches can be effective. Watch what other community groups are doing to promote activities and adopt the best of these. Don't overlook the potential of this type of promotional activity. The worst a business can say is "no," and it is always worthwhile to ask.

Many of the services offered to interest parents will also interest other adults, but some additional services can be very helpful to people teaching young children and those working in other community agencies. With the phenomenal growth in child care in the United States, there has been a dramatic increase in the number of people employed in this field. Many people working in child care have not had the opportunity for formal training. They may know little about children's books and reading, and high turnover among staff makes this a continuing problem. Many early childhood and elementary education programs do not require a children's literature course with the result that many certified teachers do not have a broad knowledge of children's books or an understanding of what qualities make a book good and how trade books can be used to teach and expand reading skills. They also may not be aware of the resources of the public or school library. Health care and social service workers likewise are likely unaware of library resources for children on topics such as hospitalization, nutrition, adoption, or divorce.

To serve teachers of young children, libraries can take a two-prong approach. First, they can work to see that service is readily available to child care facilities and that staff are encouraged to use the library. Second, the library can offer in-service training on topics relating to children's materials and library service.

Encourage all child care facilities to use the public library. Many child care programs have few books and lack the money to purchase them. If the public library provides bookmobile service or a special book circulation program for child care centers, be sure that all the facilities in the service area know about the service. Make contact with child care programs, preferably with a personal visit or contact or at least with an attractive mailing. Many young children are in family day care homes, and efforts should also be made to reach these providers. Explain how library materials can be used to enrich the curriculum and to introduce children to books. Ask how the library could best help them in their work with children. One library discovered

that day care centers were unable to use library audiovisual resources because of lack of equipment. As part of a special project to reach young children in child care they assigned someone to work with centers, developed deposit collections, and purchased audiovisual equipment for loan. Many libraries provide special programs for groups as part of their regular services either at the library or in the child care center.

Library policies often discourage day care centers and other groups from borrowing library materials. For example, policies that allow a library to issue cards only to individuals make a teacher personally responsible for any damages. Even with an institutional card, fear of being charged for damages when there is no money in the budget for this keeps many child care centers from using libraries regularly. In order to get child care programs to use the library, it may be necessary to develop some special policies. With an ever-increasing number of young children in full day care, this is where many young children are today, and it may be the only way the library will reach them.

The library can help child care teachers and workers to develop skills by offering training on techniques of reading to children, by selecting appropriate books, and by showing the variety of materials for both children and adults in the library. Many child care programs have regular staff training scheduled and would be receptive to a presentation geared to their needs by the library. A workshop could include examples of how good children's books can be used for curriculum-related activities. Show concept books and a selection of picture books reflective of the variety available at the library. Stress that use of books should not be limited to curriculum topics because reading books that children enjoy teaches them that books are fun and helps with reading readiness. Introduce resources from the library that can help teachers such as subject bibliographies, books of fingerplays, flannelboard stories, puppetry, and songs. Talk about nonprint materials that can be checked out. By subscribing to one or more periodicals directed at teachers of young children, especially one that gives practical ideas for activities, the library will have something especially for their use. Explain library services available to teachers and groups of children. In situations where child care staff experience with books is limited, offering to do a short series

FIGURE 9. Working with child care centers is an effective way to reach children. Here a librarian introduces a box of books to a child care center director. (Richland County [SC] Public Library)

of story hours can help get them started in making reading part of the daily routine.

The library can also hold a workshop at the library for staff from several centers at one time. However, scheduling can be a problem since it is hard to get people to come after work and hard for staff to get away during the day. Some libraries mail short monthly or quarterly newsletters to child care centers which include book ideas, a nature or art activity taken from a library resource, and some books helpful for the teachers. By using a variety of tactics and letting those teaching young children know that the library is there and wants to help, the library can foster the idea that it is a community resource. This can increase use by child care centers and reach children who may not get to the library.

Be sure other agencies and organizations know about library resources for children through booklists and personal contacts. Health departments, clinics, hospitals, and doctors would find it

helpful to know about books on diseases, hospitals, drugs, alcohol, and other medically related topics. Scouting organizations can be made aware of resources on crafts and the outdoors. Other organizations may be interested in knowing about resources on adoption, being in a single-parent family, death, stamp collecting, and other topics related to their function. Public libraries are still used by a relatively small segment of the population: the more libraries do to inform people about resources, the more likely they are to expand that base. As the library builds relationships with more community groups, opportunities for shared activities may develop. The library may be able to do booklists of children's books to go with a local museum special exhibit; a dance, music, or drama event for children; or a hospital health fair.

Library media specialists work with teachers as a basic part of service and have the advantage of a more limited population with which to work. However, many media specialists wish teachers made better use of the media center and its resources. By regularly helping teachers pull resources together on a topic they make them more aware of the value of the media center. A special shelf of books suggested for reading aloud in classes may be helpful as would preparing a regular newsletter to highlight new and topical materials in the media center. Getting faculty excited about children's books and library resources will result in students being more interested in the library as well.

It is impossible for any librarian to get to know and work closely with every child in his or her service area. By putting emphasis on reaching those who work and live directly with children, libraries can have the potential of reaching many more children than they can reach directly. Since those whom children know best can have the most influence on them, this is a powerful tool for reaching children that many libraries leave untapped. By reaching out into the community, the library can use these other adults to help turn children on to reading and the library.

SPECIAL PUBLICATIONS FOR TEACHERS AND PARENTS

The growth of early childhood education programs has lead to publication of several periodicals focusing on ideas and activities which are directed at teachers and parents but which librarians will also find useful themselves. They contain such things as fingerplays, flannelboard stories and patterns, songs, and crafts. Among those available are:

Building Blocks (3893 Brindle Wood, Elgin, Il 60120). 10 issues/year.
> Available in a family edition and a Child Care Edition which has several extra pages. Format is a half-size newspaper. Includes rhymes, ideas to teach concepts, book ideas, paper fun activities.

The Good Apple Paper (Good Apple, Inc., Box 299, Carthedge, IL 62321-0299). 6 issues/year.
> Large newspaper-sized format makes it harder to read than others, but it has lots of good ideas for both preschool and elementary teachers.

Kidstuff (1307 South Killian Drive, Lake Park, FL 33403). 12 issues/year.
> Each issue focuses on a theme and includes rhymes, flannelboard stories, book and activity suggestions.

Parent's Choice (Box 185, Waban MA 02168). Quarterly.
> Focuses on books for children but includes articles on films, videotapes, television, etc.

Totline (Totline Press, 1004 Harborview Lane, Everett, WA 98203). 6 issues/year.

> Activities in art, creative movement, learning games, science, nutrition, and language plus thematic and seasonal ideas.

BIBLIOGRAPHY

Association for Library Service to Children. *Programming to Introduce Adults to Children's Literature.* Program Support Publications #3. Chicago: American Library Association, 1981.

Botel, Morton. "How to Help Young Children to Read." Prelude, Series 6. New York: Children's Book Council, 1981 (cassette).

Browder, Rusty, Barbara Eckhoff, and Priscilla L. Moulton. "Community Cooperation to Encourage Reading." Prelude, Series 6. New York: Children's Book Council, 1981 (cassette).

Butler, Dorothy. *Babies Need Books.* New York: Atheneum, 1980.

Butler, Dorothy and Marie Clay. *Reading Begins at Home; Preparing Children for Reading Before They Go to School.* Exeter, NH: Heinemann, 1982.

Children in Action. (Part 1 Come and See—Overview; Part 2 Know and Think—Cognitive Development; Part 3 Laugh and Cry— Emotional Development; Part 4 Meet and Greet—Social Development; Part 5 Move and Do—Physical Development. Library Video Network, 1984 (videotapes).
> This series provides basic information about child development and shows how books and libraries can contribute to growth.

Cooperman, Paul. *Taking Books to Heart: How to Develop a Love of Reading in Your Child.* Reading, MA: Addison-Wesley, 1986.

Denniston, Susan. *Library Child Care Link: Linking with the Child Care Community.* Santa Clara, CA: South Bay Cooperative Library System, 1985.
> This manual is based on a day care-library project.

Hearne, Betsy. *Sharing Books with Young Children.* Chicago: American Library Association, 1986 (videotape).

Johnson, Ferne, ed. *Start Early for an Early Start.* Preschool Services and Parent Education Committee, Children's Services Division, American Library Association. Chicago: American Library Association, 1976.

Larrick, Nancy. "You Can't Start Too Soon: Books and Reading for the Preschool Child." Prelude, Series 3. New York: Children's Book Council, 1977 (cassette).

Oppenheim, Joanne, et al. *Choosing Books for Kids: How to Choose the Right Book for the Right Child at the Right Time.* New York: Ballantine, 1986.

Reed, Arthea. *Comics to Classics: A Parent's Guide to Books for Teens and Preteens.* Newark, DE: International Reading Association, 1988.

Russ, Lavinia. "Encouraging Families to Read Together." Prelude, Series 2. New York: Children's Book Council, 1976 (cassette).

Trelease, Jim. *The Read Aloud Handbook.* Rev. ed. New York: Penguin, 1985.

———. *Turning On the Turned-Off Reader.* Springfield, MA: Jim Trelease, 1983 (cassette).

What's So Great about Books. Orlando, FL: Orlando Public Library, 1976 (16mm film).

Administration of Children's Services

Administration involves the functions of planning, supervising, training, evaluating, reporting, budgeting, and coordinating. Administration of library services to children means managing services to children so that they continue to operate smoothly while moving forward to improve services. It involves all the many duties children's librarians, branch librarians, coordinators, or media specialists may do in addition to the daily activities of their work. Administration encompasses what is done in addition to the routines of preparing for and carrying out programs, teaching library skills, selecting and weeding materials, helping children and adults find books, and other tasks that fill the day. Often the daily routines of the library can keep staff so busy that it is easy to allow no time for management activities even though these are very important.

In recent years, more and more librarians serving children have recognized their need for management skills in order to do their job well and to increase the status of children's services in libraries. Too often librarians working with children have been taken less seriously than those working in other areas of public libraries. This has been due both to the lower status given to people who work with children generally and to the perception that children's librarians spend their time having fun and cutting and pasting. Children's librarians have often not recognized themselves, and communicated to others, the managerial skills involved in planning and executing an active program of service to children. The result has been that, for many people, children's services was a dead end professionally.

Increased awareness of and use of management skills can bring both increased respect and more opportunities for advancement into management for those who so desire.

The administrative structure of children's services in libraries and media centers depends on the size and organizational structure of the library or system. In larger libraries, there is usually a coordinator who acts as manager for children's services either full time or in addition to public service responsibilities. Children's librarians within the system are responsible for their particular libraries. In smaller libraries, many school districts, or in outlets of larger systems, a single individual is often responsible for all phases of services to children either at one library or in several locations. Branch staff may be generalists with children just one of their responsibilities. In very small public libraries, the director may also be responsible for services to children. In some schools a teacher, rather than a library media specialist, must also function as the librarian, or the library is run by an aide with one librarian responsible for several libraries. In these situations, it is even easier to push aside managing in favor of daily tasks.

However, knowledge of administration is necessary to all librarians. Daily activities must be balanced with planning and evaluating. Anyone responsible for any library function needs to utilize management processes to do the best job possible, to prepare for the future, and to keep the director and the rest of the staff knowledgeable about department activities and functions.

In their roles as managers, librarians working with children need to develop good management skills. They need to have goals, objectives, and strategies mapped out to change and improve services. This means they need to be able to think, plan, and anticipate rather than just doing things as they have always been done or as a predecessor did them. In order to improve services they need to be able to examine programs or projects with a fresh, critical eye. To be good managers, librarians need to be able to develop creative solutions and new approaches to challenges and problems. This often involves considerable imagination and creativity because library budgetary resources are often limited. A good manager does not suggest change for change's sake or to stir up staff but should be willing to challenge tradition and suggest changes and innovations to improve services. Good managers are not afraid of controversy when they believe it will result in improvements. At the same time, good managers know how to work with others and are aware of individual staff temperaments and differences so that they are able to bring people together rather than creating unnecessary staff resistance to evaluation and change.

Good managers can look at their areas of responsibility and see the big picture rather than focusing on all its individual parts. They can look at their areas of responsibility critically and consider strengths and weaknesses and make suggestions for improvement and changes. Good management in library service to children also means being an advocate for excellence in library service to children within the library, school, community, and profession.

PLANNING

Planning is a way of looking toward the future. It involves seeing where the library is now, deciding where it should be, and outlining the way to get there. *Planning and Role Setting in Public Libraries* (1987) details a methodology for planning that establishes library roles and priorities as a basis for setting goals. Evaluation through output measures provides data for future planning. This book and its companion volume, *Output Measures for Public Libraries* (1987), are valuable resources for librarians.

Seeing planning as a necessary process for each library has led the American Library Association to move away from developing quantitative standards for service to various age levels because they do not allow for individual community needs. Some states have written guidelines or standards for children's services that detail what minimums are necessary for quality service. As part of the process of rethinking their approach to standards, the American Library Association had committees develop working papers on goals and guidelines for services by age levels. Although published in 1973, the statement developed by the Task Force on Children's Services remains a useful philosophical statement of what services for children should include. It stresses equal access and availability of full library services for children, staff development, planning, including interdepartmental planning and planning with other community agencies, and evaluation.

Planning involves both short-term and long-term thinking. Plans should be realistic and attainable and not dreams which staff are unlikely to have time or money to implement. Planning is also not something done once and never changed; rather it is an ongoing process. Good librarians write goals and objectives and then change and modify them as situations change or new needs develop.

To develop a long-range plan, librarians need to look at what needs exist relating to service to children and then determine needs the library can best meet. This is called needs assessment. This process involves self-analysis as well as statistical and other evaluations. Librarians should look at services as an outsider would see them. Evaluate what is seen on entering the children's area or media center and what it looks like through the eyes of children of varying ages. Assess the quality of reference and reader's advisory services. Is there someone on duty who really knows the children's collection whenever the library is open? Evaluate the working relationships the library has with other local libraries and media centers. Make lists of all things staff and others find frustrating or wish were different. List the projects or changes that staff members have wanted to implement previously but haven't.

Planning should not be done in isolation by a single staff member. Supervisors or administrators, branch staff, and support staff should be consulted and involved. In schools, teachers and administrators should be included in planning. Involving a group of parents and children will add user input and suggestions to the process. In libraries where there is a children's coordinator, all children's librarians should have opportunities for input. Even if one staff member is responsible for planning, involvement of others will result in different viewpoints and support for the results. Changes recommended for one department may affect other areas as well. For example, if the plan involves a reallocation of a librarian's time, the administration needs to be supportive of this. Any goals and objectives set for library service to children must be consistent with overall goals of the library or school.

Another aspect of planning is learning as much as possible about the service area and what is available for children there. This helps focus on community needs that the library may be able to meet. Determine the population by age group to learn how many children there are under age five, from five to nine and so on. Examine the population by ethnic group and economic and educational levels. States publish statistical summaries that provide information by geographic areas. Local and county planning offices and school districts may also have this information. Otherwise, population data are available from census reports. If the state or school districts use standardized tests, find out how children in the service area perform on readiness and school achievement tests. This may affect materials selection. Determine community characteristics and resources such as public and private schools; child development centers and family day care homes; recreational and cultural facilities; churches, synagogues, and other religious institutions; businesses and industries; organizations for children such as scouts or Boys' Clubs; athletic and activity programs such as team sports; dance and music schools; and organizations that may be resources for people, funding, or programming assistance. In large systems or those covering both rural and town or urban areas, these resources should be determined for each branch or outlet service area.

Good planning should include community input. A survey of children and parents may reveal materials or services they think the library lacks or what they think of library activities. A one-day survey in the community or at a shopping center could give valuable information on what people use or do not use in the library or the children's area. Asking different groups and organizations what they would like to see the library do for children

can also be helpful. Whether you incorporate community input or not, keep the focus of planning on what will benefit children and adults in using the children's area of libraries rather than on library and staff needs alone.

Be realistic about what the department can accomplish: undertaking too many new projects will only lead to frustration. A major project or decision to emphasize certain services may even mean eliminating or cutting back on other activities at least temporarily.

Examine how time is currently allocated. List all the major responsibilities and tasks of the department and how much time is devoted to each. Determine the amount of time used for public service, collection development, programmming for each age group, displays, teaching library skills, public relations, and professional reading. Evaluate whether the library has its various activities in the right proportions. If the library does so many programs that staff members never have time to undertake new projects, then the library may be overextending itself. If the library has many requests from preschool centers for programs and doing them leaves no time to do programs for older children, who may be more difficult to attract, programming priorities may be out of proportion. Needs not being met should be considered in planning. While it is difficult to limit activities for which there is demand, when staff is limited, it may be necessary to set a maximum amount of time for a service and stick to it.

Planning and the setting of goals and objectives forces staff to think about how to accomplish a desired end and how to break it down into manageable steps. Goals are broad statements of desired results. Objectives list specific targets within goals. Objectives should be specific and measurable whenever possible. Based on goals and objectives, strategies set out specific steps to meet objectives. Following is an example of goals, objectives, and strategies.

Goal: To increase the number of children using the library.

> **Objective 1: To increase by 20 percent the number of children using the library.**
>
> > *Strategy 1:* Visit every school in service area. Make contact with each library media specialist and principal. If possible, talk with children in assembly or classes.

Strategy 2: Design a flyer to give to all school children which emphasizes the library as both a resource and a fun place.

Objective 2: To increase the number of children having library cards by 15 percent.

Strategy 1: Actively encourage all children coming to the library to get a library card.

Strategy 2: Arrange with teachers bringing class groups to have applications completed and returned before visits so that cards can be distributed during the visit.

Strategy 3: Develop a small incentive to get children to come back to the library on their own within one month.

Objective 3: To increase the number and variety of programs for children ages 6 to 10 and achieve a 25 percent increase in attendance per program for this age group.

Strategy 1: Do one special program every month throughout the year.

Strategy 2: Form an advisory panel of children to provide a sounding board and to give ideas of programs.

Strategy 3: Improve publicity for programs by printing flyers for each program and distributing them in schools and community, and by working to improve publicity in community newsletters as well as the newspaper and other media.

While planning may seem to be a lot of trouble and paperwork, developing clearly laid out goals and objectives makes it easier to make changes. Planning is a starting point, and it is not of much value if plans are not implemented and evaluated.

SUPERVISION

Supervising is the process of directing and overseeing and should be thought of as a way to help all staff provide better service. The head of the department must supervise other staff. In larger libraries, the coordinator may supervise staff who work with children in numerous branches. Similarly, a school district media services coordinator of a school district supervises the library in each school. Frequently a branch children's librarian or library media specialist walks a delicate balance between an immediate supervisor such as the branch head or principal and a supervisor from their specialty. Often the direct supervisor is the person on site, and the other person has indirect authority, acting as an advisor.

Supervision involves scheduling staff to ensure all services are done well. Developing a realistic schedule involves planning time for programs, public service duty, and materials selection as well as scheduling time for planning and special projects. In libraries time management is always difficult because the highest priority must be serving the public, and this is something that does not fit into schedules. An unexpected group in the library or a rush of people takes priority over other tasks. However, schedules help to ensure time is allocated for all activities and to monitor what is actually done. It makes staff accountable for their time and helps to minimize time that slips away. It also gives the librarian valuable information about how time is spent to use in reporting and planning.

Scheduling should provide for adequate coverage of public service as well as completion of all necessary routines. In libraries with more than one staff member serving children, there should be someone working in the public service area at all times. In smaller libraries where a single staff member has to be away from the area to do programs and other activities, other staff should assume the responsibility for helping children. Where a children's area is in a separate room or on a separate floor, it is essential for good service to have staff working in the area at all times. Work can be done at a public service desk as long as it is the type of task that allows staff to remain alert to activity in the area. In a school library media center, schedules are often determined by classes and other groups of children, but every effort should be made to retain enough flexibility so that the library and the librarian are available to individual users as well.

A good schedule also helps set reasonable limits on what staff can and cannot do. It is better to do fewer things well than many projects and activities haphazardly. Schedules help prioritize tasks and eliminate what is unnecessary. They help ensure that all necessary routines are completed and that less enjoyable ones are not allowed to go undone. A good example of a routine often pushed aside for lack of time is shelf reading. However, if shelvers or other staff are scheduled even 15 minutes a day shelf reading, and if they consistently work their way around the collection, the shelves will stay in good order.

Time management is also part of supervision. This means monitoring how time is used and knowing how long it should reasonably take to do a specific job. Examples of tasks that can be measured to determine time required are shelving and shelf reading. Librarians should know how long it takes to set up and shelve a cart of children's nonfiction, fiction, and picture books so that they know what to expect of staff responsible for shelving. If personnel are expected to straighten shelves or shelf read at the same time, allow for this. Applying similar approaches to other tasks will help determine appropriate time frames for them.

Avoid putting off the tasks which are less enjoyable or which seem to be overwhelming. Deal with paperwork immediately instead of rehandling it several times. In the same way, handle staff problems or questions as they come up rather than putting off making decisions or dealing with problems. Large projects can be broken down into a series of steps with a timetable for each. Avoid getting preoccupied with details. Learn to decide what is important and what is not. For example, quick, effective displays are better than ones which require lots of preparation time. Sharing them among several branches is more efficient than using them once. If name tags are made for programs, choose a simple design for a series rather than a unique one each week. When there are busywork projects such as cutting, counting things out, or folding, involve children who enjoy helping.

Supervisors also need to see that all necessary routines are completed and that less enjoyable ones are not allowed to lapse. By managing time well service to children will be better and staff will feel better about their work because they will better be able to see what has been accomplished.

In addition to scheduling and monitoring staff, supervisors are responsible for ensuring the quality of service by monitoring not only what staff is doing but also how well it is being done. This involves observing programs, reader's advisory and reference services, and other services to be sure staff is performing up to expectations. The effective supervisor does this with the overall goal of improving service and helping staff rather than to maintain control over all activities. Staff should know what is expected of them. Good supervisors use what they observe as the tool for recognizing specific staff needs for training and assistance and as occasions for praise and reinforcement. They accentuate the positive things staff are doing on a regular basis but deal with problem areas directly.

It is better to talk over problems as they are observed and, with the staff involved, work out a plan or approach to solve the problem. Staff problems can range from consistent lateness to failure to perform tasks or ignoring suggestions. Whether minor or serious, they need to be dealt with in a straightforward fashion. Staff also needs to feel free to talk to supervisors about problems with their work without worrying that this will be thrown back at them later. Developing open communication with staff will lead to healthy working relationships.

Good supervisors also make maximum use of staff talents and skills by delegating responsibility and involving staff in planning and decision making. When people are involved in planning programs and setting goals, they will be more interested in carrying them out successfully.

TRAINING

Training gives staff the skills needed to do their jobs well. It is an ongoing process. There are always new ideas, approaches, and topics to learn about through professional reading and continuing education opportunities such as workshops, library conventions, and classes. Various staff members, including support staff, should have the opportunity to attend meetings, rather than the head of the department always going. A summary report that can be shared with other staff should be required. If there are staff working with children who lack needed skills, supervisors should ensure that they have opportunities for training.

Training and continuing education can take many forms. Staff may take courses for credit at a college or university, perhaps working toward a master's degree or additional credentials. Workshops are offered by state libraries, library associations, universities, and other libraries. Education organizations, such as the International Reading Association and the National Association for the Education of Young Children, may have meetings or workshops that will be valuable to librarians. Other workshops in planning, management, and public relations will provide helpful information to librarians.

In-service training can also be provided by the library. Some states have children's consultants at the state library and library media center consultants in the education department who can provide training and assistance. Larger libraries with a coordinator regularly provide this kind of in-service training. Some have a formal training program where new staff are exposed to different areas of library service, the library philosophy, and procedures. Others require new children's librarians to read a certain number of specific books over a year or more to ensure a common basic knowledge of children's literature. School media specialists are usually required to participate in in-service programs sponsored by their district but often find it more difficult to attend other workshops when school is in session.

Films, videotapes, and cassettes are available on topics such as storytelling, reader's advisory work, child development, and other aspects of children's services. For example, the Children's Book Council has produced sets of cassette tapes using the series title "Prelude" on various aspects of children's books and their use with children. The American Library Association has produced some useful videotapes. These are an excellent way to provide some in-service training for staff.

All librarians working with children should read library periodicals regularly. They should read as much as possible on children's services, as well as general library periodicals to keep aware of what is happening in libraries outside of the specialty. Periodicals about serving children that should be read regularly include the *Journal of Youth Services* (formerly *Top of the News*), *Horn Book*, *School Library Journal*, and *School Library Media Quarterly*. Despite its name *School Library Journal* has many articles relating directly to public library service. *Public Libraries*, published by the Public Library Association, *American Libraries* and *Wilson Library Bulletin* are examples of general periodicals that include articles on children's books or services as well as on management and other library issues. Other periodicals such as *Library Quarterly* and *Library Trends* occasionally have articles or issues relating to services to children. Education periodicals such as *Instructor* include articles on children's books and their use. Also, periodicals such as *Parents*, which the public library probably receives, have articles helpful in understanding children and their growth and development. Be alert for articles which could be helpful to staff who may not read these periodicals regularly. There are also many

good books on children's literature and reading and on aspects of service to children. Try to read as many of these as possible, and encourage other staff to read them also.

Librarians working with children should share their knowledge about children's books with others on the staff. They can mention books to others that are likely to be particularly useful or popular. Establish regular times to review children's books for other staff. In 15 or 20 minutes, a librarian can brief other staff such as branch librarians or reference staff on a good number of new books. This is important if they help children at times the children's librarian is unavailable. In the same way, library media specialists can review books for teachers to make them aware of what is in the library and encourage reading aloud in the classroom. Enthusiasm for children's books can inspire other staff to start reading them, and, in any case, it will help them do a better job in serving children.

Although workshops and courses are important, some of the best training comes from librarians' efforts to develop and maintain the skills of their staffs and themselves. Make the atmosphere in your area one which encourages learning by all staff. Use staff meetings as an opportunity to discuss readings or issues in library service. Libraries where staff are learning are ones that are willing to step out and try something new to improve services to children.

BUDGETING

Another administrative responsibility is budgeting for the department. The costs in running the children's area or media center include staff, materials, programming, and equipment and supplies. Fiscal years begin at different times, depending on the governmental structure, and administrators begin planning financial needs for the next year well in advance. Know when administrators begin work on the budget, and, at that time, inform them of needs for the new budget year. This should be done with a written budget that can be used by the administrator in budget preparation. The budget should list the amounts of money needed for each area of operations with facts and figures and reasons to justify each item or program. Know in what form the departmental budget should be prepared and what documentation is required.

In some public libraries, the children's services budget for branches is the responsibility of the children's services head; more often it is prepared by the branch or extension department. In this case, the branch children's librarian or children's coordinator should provide input to those preparing branch budgets. School library media specialists should work to see that materials for the library are a separate budget item and not part of a larger supply budget, where they can get used for other school needs.

In submitting budget requests, remember that they are requests. Administrators and boards have to juggle all needs and requests in deciding what to include in a budget request. When the final budget has been set by the governing authority or by millage receipts, what the department receives may not match the request. However, well-justified requests will help the department get the monies it needs.

It is important for children's librarians to find out as soon as possible exactly how much money has been allocated in each category in the budget because this knowledge determines how to proceed with spending. It is their responsibility also to monitor spending so that expenditures are distributed over the year and all monies are expended without exceeding the budget. In cases where grant money is anticipated, plans for spending should be complete before receipt. Often grant money comes with a short time allowed for expenditure, and libraries which have orders prepared and waiting find themselves better able to utilize additional funds wisely.

EVALUATION

Evaluation provides the opportunity to analyze what has been done. It helps determine strengths, weaknesses, and areas needing improvement. It also provides necessary information for budget justification in requests for increased dollars for staff, materials, space, and equipment. Without evaluation and analysis, it is difficult to justify budget increases. There are two types of evaluation, both of which are important to use. Statistical evaluation provides facts and numbers. Descriptive evaluation involves comments, opinions, and analyses by staff, factors that cannot be measured, and anecdotes, comments, and letters from parents and children.

Children's librarians have often shied away from statistical evaluation, questioning how it is possible to measure a program's effect on a child or the impact a special book has on one child as compared to the impact of twenty books on another. However, administrators and government officials want numbers or hard facts and not just descriptions of success. Combining statistical and descriptive evaluation can provide a fairly comprehensive analysis of children's services. Circulation, program attendance, and the number of children using the library are important although they are not the complete story. Most state library agencies publish some type of statistical summary which allows comparison of use and expenditures with other libraries of similar size in any one state.

Evaluation must be tied into the goals and objectives for service to children. There are some standard statistical measurements, but others should relate to how well the department met its goals for the year. If it did not meet all objectives or if it exceeded them, evaluations need to analyze why.

Statistical evaluation has been increasingly recognized as necessary for libraries. The American Library Association's *Planning and Role Setting in Public Libraries* (1987) emphasizes the need for evaluation using statistical output measures. These output measures which are standardized indicators of services provided are explained in *Output Measures for Public Libraries* (Van House et al., 1987). This book suggests a methodology for calculating a number of measurements which show how the community is using the library, such as circulation per capita, program attendance per capita, and in-library use of materials per capita. It also explains how to take these measures in a library. However, this book does not provide any guidelines for information specifically relating to children's services. Indeed there are some output measures that are difficult to apply to children's services because they involve surveys. It is hard to survey children who may not be able to read a form or fully understand questions about user satisfaction even if they are reworded. Also, children are less sophisticated in knowing what they want from the library or what the library should be expected to provide.

Nevertheless, there is much that can be used by those serving children. Most basic is the philosophy which puts emphasis on library output such as performance and contribution to the community rather than to input, such as amount of money, number of books added, number of staff, or what comes into the library. Using this approach, service is not evaluated on the number of books added to the collection but in the use made of materials.

A pilot project in Wisconsin has tested adaptations of output measures for measuring children's services. The output measures tested were:

1. Juvenile circulation per juvenile capita
2. In-library use of juvenile materials per juvenile capita
3. Juvenile library visits per juvenile capita
4. Annual juvenile program attendance per juvenile capita
5. Reference fill rate for juveniles
6. Library registration of juveniles as a percentage of juvenile population
7. Turnover rate of juvenile materials

In order to calculate several of these, it is necessary to know the number of children in the library's service area or school. To look at an individual branch's performance, use the number of children in that branch's service area. Decide if the library will keep separate statistics on adults using the children's area.

For a statistic such as program attendance, record attendance at each program during the year and divide the total by the child population. Record the number of programs and attendance by age group to determine where you are reaching the most children. Also useful are statistics for in-library versus out-of-library programming. Here is an example using the library programs of a main library and two branches.

Type of program	# of programs	Total Attendance	Average Attendance
In-library programs, ages 3-5	75	1,650	22
In-library programs, ages 6-9	30	900	30
In-library programs, ages 10-12	6	65	10.8
Out-of-library programs			
Day care programs	150	4,500	30
Spring festival	1	750	—
Totals	262	7,865	

When you consider that the total number of children in the service area ages 0 to 13 was 9,400, then 7,865/9,400 = .83, which is the program attendance per capita.

From this, cost per child attending can be calculated by using costs for each program and dividing by the number of children attending. To get an estimated figure for how many different children attended at least one program, use a sampling technique.

It is not possible to keep track of all desired statistics 52 weeks a year. For example, if a public library records circulation of children's materials separately from circulation of adult materials, it is no problem to get a total of children's materials circulated. If it is not kept separately, there will be no record of children's books circulated. In the same way, most libraries do not maintain daily statistics on in-house use of materials. *Output Measures for Public Libraries* explains clearly how to do a sampling to get good estimates. This technique can be used to measure any service which is fairly regular, but it is not recommended for services such as programming, which may be less regular and where it is easy enough to count or give a good estimate each time.

To take a sample, the book suggests using a week in either April or October during which staff counts whatever use it wants to measure. For example, if a library is counting children's reference questions, and the percentage successfully completed, including reader's advisory questions, tally these for a week. Multiply by 50 to allow for days during the year that the library is closed. The Wisconsin project used this method. However, since children's use varies a great deal between summer and the rest of the year, children's services measurements require some adjustment. It would be more accurate to take a tally one week in April or October as suggested and during one week in the middle of the summer. Using this approach would mean multiplying the spring or fall sample times 40 weeks and the summer sample by 10 weeks and adding these together. The number of weeks in each category can be adjusted by the number of weeks a library calculates as summer weeks. Per capita use is figured by dividing the total by the number of children in the service area. This same procedure can be used to figure juvenile circulation and in-library use. For the latter, ask patrons not to re-shelve books or other materials they read or use in the library during sampling weeks. School library media centers can use the same techniques by adjusting the number of weeks to fit the school year.

As a library begins this process, it establishes a baseline against which the next year's performance can be measured. It allows the library to compare past and present performance and to establish goals for the future. Because calculations produce a ratio, the figures are adjusted for population size.

Use statistics to verify yearly objectives as well. If, for example, one of the objectives was to increase juvenile registrations by 20 percent, determine the total number registered at the beginning of the year and keep track of the number who register during the year. By figuring the percent increase, the objective can be measured.

Statistical evaluation, however, is not in itself sufficient. Descriptive or narrative evaluation provides a way to analyze statistical findings. There may be reasons for or suppositions about certain trends. There may be an explanation as to why an objective was not accomplished or why it was exceeded. This is also the place to report things that cannot be covered by statistics, such as the librarian's personal feelings about a series of programs or a new project. For example, the staff may feel that a new program, though not well attended, was worthwhile because of the response of those who did attend. It provides an opportunity to convey the flavor of services and a department to others.

Another necessary type of evaluation is a complete analysis of the department to provide a basis for planning or to make recommendations for major change. This should include evaluating the physical appearance of the area including attractiveness and adequacy of space for all functions and accessibility to the disabled. It should include an evaluation of the collection, programming, staff, and public relations of the department. It should also include analysis of how adequately the library reaches the children in the service area. As strengths and weaknesses are identified, it will be necessary to prioritize needs and concentrate on one or two areas at a time. In any case, the process of evaluation leads to needs assessment which leads full circle back to planning. Planning and evaluation are naturally intertwined and one is not really possible without the other.

REPORTING

Reporting informs others about what the children's department or media center is doing. With staff focused on their own jobs, they may not know everything that the children's department or library media center is doing unless librarians take time to tell them.

Reporting to administrators or supervisors regularly keeps them informed. It also keeps library service to children in their minds regularly, not just when there is a problem or need. Reports are also an excellent way to make administrators or supervisors aware of problems and needs as they develop and prepare them gradually for any new requests. They can also be useful for administrators or supervisors to use in summarizing library activities to the board and community.

It is a good idea to prepare a short, written monthly report discussing what has been done and giving statistics on use and special activities. Annually, there should be a more extensive report including the statistics and analysis of the year as well as a summarization of the year. This is essentially the department evaluation. In reporting it is helpful to include any anecdotes or interesting things that happened in the department, comments by parents or children, or anything else that is illustrative of the department's activities. This helps to humanize a report and give the flavor as well as information about services.

Although it is not necessary to report formally to other staff, it is important to keep them aware of activities and important developments. This fosters good communication and offers an opportunity for others to express concerns or opinions. It also helps other staff to understand the purposes and functions of library service to children.

SUMMARY

The real challenge for children's librarians is to take all the parts of managing a department and make them fit together, along with other tasks, to create a smooth-running and effective operation. Coordinating all the different responsibilities is a challenge whatever the size and staff of the library. With the pressures just to get daily tasks done and meet programming requests and obligations, it is easy to forget about managing or to dismiss it as unnecessary, especially when the library is small or has no coordinator to oversee services. However, use of management tools allows librarians to analyze and plan activities, making it possible for children's services to develop and grow in an orderly, planned way.

BIBLIOGRAPHY

Alvarez, Robert S. *Library Boss: Thoughts on Library Personnel.* San Francisco, CA: Administrator's Digest Press, 1987.

American Association of School Librarians and Association for Educational Communications and Technology. *Information Power: Guidelines for School Library Media Programs.* Chicago: American Library Association, 1988.

Chelton, Mary K. "Evaluation of Children's Services." *Library Trends* 35 (Winter 1987): 463-484.

Coughlin, Caroline M. "Children's Librarians: Managing in the Midst of Myths." *School Library Journal* 24 (Jan 1978): 15-18.

Gault, Robin. "Performance Measures for Evaluating Public Library Children's Services." *Public Libraries* 25 (Spring 1986): 134.

———. "Planning for Children's Services in Public Libraries." *Public Libraries* 25 (Summer 1986): 60.

Gervasi, Anne and Betty Kay Seibt. *Handbook for Small, Rural, and Emerging Public Libraries.* Phoenix, AZ: Oryx Press, 1988.

Ivy, Barbara A. "Developing Managerial Skills in Children's Librarians. *Library Trends* 35 (Winter 1987): 449-461.

Kingsbury, Mary E. "Goals for Children's Services in Public Libraries." *School Library Journal* 24 (Jan 1978): 19-21.

Minudri, Regina. "The Management Perspective." In *Libraries Serving Youth: Directions for Service in the 1990's.* Proceedings of New York State Conference, April 16-18, 1986. New York, Youth Services Section, New York Library Association, 1987.

Planning and Role Setting for Public Libraries: A Manual of Options and Procedures. Chicago: American Library Association, 1987.

Prostano, Emanuel and Joyce S. Prostano. *Case Studies in Library/Media Management.* Littleton, CO: Libraries Unlimited, 1982.

Robbins-Carter, Jane and Douglas L Zweizig. "Are We There Yet? Evaluating Library Collections, Reference Service, Programs, and Personnel." *American Libraries* 16-17 (Oct 1985–March 1986): 624-627, 724-727, 780-784, 32-36.

Rogus, Joseph F. "Supervisor Savvy: Strengthening Performance as a School Library Media Supervisor." *School Library Media Quarterly* 14 (Spring 1986): 133-137.

"Task Force on Children's Services Working Paper." *School Library Journal* 20 (Sept 1973): 26-27.

Van House, Nancy A. et al. *Output Measures for Public Libraries: A Manual of Standardized Procedures.* 2nd ed. Chicago: American Library Association, 1987.

Wheeler, Joseph L. *Wheeler and Goldhor's Practical Administration of Public Libraries.* Rev. by Carlton Rochell. New York: Harper and Row, 1981.

Woolls, Blanche. *Grant Proposal Writing: A Handbook for School Library Media Specialists.* New York: Greenwood Press, 1986.

Yesner, Bernice L. and Hilda L. Jay. *The School Administrator's Guide to Evaluating Library Media Programs.* Hamden, CT: Library Professional Publications, 1987.

Young, Diana. "Evaluating Children's Services." *Public Libraries* 23 (Spring 1984): 20.

———. "Output Measures for Children's Services in Wisconsin Public Libraries." *Public Libraries* 25 (Spring 1986): 30.

Zweizig, Douglas L., Joan A. Braune, and Gloria A. Waity. *Output Measures for Children's Services in Wisconsin Public Libraries: A Pilot Project—1984-85.* Unpublished LSCA (Library Services and Construction Act) project. Madison, WI, 1985.

Publicity and Public Relations

Publicizing and promoting library services in a dynamic way is essential if the community or school population is to be aware of what the library is doing and be supportive of its efforts. If a library or school district is large enough to have a public relations coordinator, the librarian may only need to give information and ideas for promotion to that person. In many libraries, however, responsibility for promoting services to children lies with children's librarians or branch librarians doing special activities. In schools it is important to promote the library media center within the school and also to the community so that the public will be aware of how it contributes to children's learning.

Public relations is just what it says: relations with the public. Public relations encompasses every aspect of a library's operations including appearance of the library, staff competence and attitudes, quality of the collections, and publicity. Public relations is what the library does to create the public's impression and awareness of the library. Publicity is what the library does to publicize special programs and events, to highlight special services, or to inform people about the library in general. Publicity can be done with posters, flyers, and other printed materials, newspaper articles, or radio and television coverage. Publicity is an important part of public relations, but it is not by itself a public relations program because the latter is a much broader concept.

In the children's area of public libraries or in a school library media center, the image projected can affect use, circulation, program attendance, and even children's behavior. Regular evaluation and monitoring of the area and service and reviewing publicity of the last several months can help librarians to see how the image can be improved.

Other staff in public libraries often feel that the children's department seems to get all the publicity. Children's services departments often find it easier to get publicity, especially pictorial coverage, than reference or other adult services. A child listening to a story or watching a puppet show is more obviously appealing than some other area of library service. This does not mean the children's department can sit back, but it may find it easier to succeed. In schools, media centers sometimes find it difficult to get their services known beyond the walls of the school. In any promotional activity, it is important to work with other staff and keep the administration informed. News releases should be approved by the administrator or individual responsible for the overall image of the library or school.

PRINTED MATERIALS

Flyers, brochures, and posters are an important way of communicating about services and programs. They can be placed at strategic locations in the service area and may reach a different audience than the newspaper. In schools, they can be posted in classrooms, cafeteria, and other areas and sent home to parents. Public libraries also find that schools are an excellent place to publicize their activities.

Bookmarks are always popular and can be used to give brief information or to generally promote reading and the library. They are easy and inexpensive to make and remind people of the message every time they open the book. Since four or five bookmarks can be made from a single 8 1/2 x 11 inch sheet of paper, the library can use four different designs, include separate information for different branches, or reproduce the same bookmark several times on each sheet of paper.

Booklists are also effective public relations tools and worth the time they take to prepare. Many children come into libraries looking for ideas of something good to read, and booklists on different genres such as mysteries or sports can be very useful. Booklists which give suggestions for other books similar to very popular titles or those by favorite authors or which focus on a type of character such as mice are also popular. Choose good quality books to include on booklists. Include both new and older titles. Booklists are a good way to promote books that may not circulate as much as librarians would like. Short one-line annotations help people select books from a list. Parents are also often looking for help in choosing books for children and will appreciate booklists. Booklists can also be used to target a particular audience outside the library. For example, place a list of books about doctors and hospitals in local doctors' offices. In schools, booklists can relate to topics in the curriculum or special activities in the school. By preparing bibliographies for teachers, library media specialists help teachers realize the value of the media center as a resource for enriching classroom learning.

In doing flyers or posters to advertise a program, activity, or type of service, or printing bookmarks or booklists, make them as attractive and professional looking as possible. Flyers with no graphics or those that look thrown together do not make a good first impression and may not be read. With the quality of advertising that people see on a daily basis, only good-looking, attention-getting materials will catch the eye. Be sure to put the library's name prominently on all printed materials.

In preparing brochures and flyers, begin by deciding what information will be included. Use only what is necessary: the more detail there is, the less likely it is that people will read it. However, be sure to include all pertinent information accurately. One of the best ways to learn what makes attractive printed materials is to start to look closely at brochures and flyers put out by other agencies, including other libraries. Pick up samples of anything attractive and try to determine what makes it catch the eye. Examine advertising and slogans in

the media. Books on library public relations offer suggestions and ideas. Some include detailed instructions on how to do professional-looking layout in terms that amateurs can understand.

If there is a person on the staff who draws well, use that talent to help with artwork. Clip-type art books and other noncopyrighted art services have illustrations which can be used freely. Many copy machines now have reducing and enlarging capabilities allowing an illustration or type to be adjusted in size. With clip art, only part of an illustration can be used, or several can be combined to get the desired effect. Pressable type, which can be transferred to artwork, is easy to use and is available in many sizes and typefaces as well as lines and graphic symbols. By using tricks of the trade such as special pencils and graph paper with nonreproducible lines, almost anyone can learn to do attractive layouts. A good art supply store carries lettering and other materials, such as books of attractive borders, which can help make the library's materials more effective in promoting library services. Computer graphics programs open up even more possibilities.

Do not use copyrighted illustrations from books or printed materials without getting written permission from the publisher. To do so violates copyright laws. Publishers of children's books will frequently give permission to use an illustration but may put restrictions on its use and require the library to give credit for the illustration. To request permission to use an illustration, write to the children's book editor or library promotions director, giving author, title, and illustrator, and explain briefly exactly how it will be used, how many copies will be made and to whom the flyer, booklist, or whatever will be distributed. This requires time so it is necessary to plan ahead. Names and addresses can be found in *Literary Marketplace*.

Flyers, brochures, and other printed materials are only useful if they reach the intended audience. Public libraries need to place materials in appropriate community locations as well as in several areas of the library. By putting copies of printed materials at social service and health agency offices, schools, day care facilities, doctors' offices, churches, recreation departments, and other community locations, they are more likely to be seen by people who do not use the library. Often permission to distribute any information in the schools is required from the administration, and time must be allowed for this. Getting publicity into the home that can be put on the refrigerator or bulletin board increases the chance that families will remember a special activity or service. Do not limit flyers about children's department activities to that area of the library because some parents will not see them there. Library media centers have the advantage of captive audiences and can put information in each classroom and ask teachers to help promote the library.

NEWSPAPERS

News releases about activities and services for children help attract people to a program or exhibit and also inform people in the community about what the library is doing. There is an art to writing successful news releases. Paragraphs and sentences should be short and concise. Include all essential information in the first paragraph: who, what, when, where, and how. This way the first paragraph can be used on radio as well, and it helps to ensure the newspaper does not cut essential information. It also ensures that the person who doesn't read an entire article gets the essential information. In additional paragraphs, provide other information about the program or service to give a clearer idea what to expect. Do not keep writing just to send out a long release, but do include anything important or particularly interesting. Put information in descending order of importance so that if the article is cut, it will be the least important information that is not included.

News releases should be typed double-spaced, and triple-spaced between paragraphs. Use only one side of the paper, and don't let paragraphs run over from one page to the next. Allow plenty of margin for editors' notations. Proofread very carefully, especially all names, dates, and times. At the top of the page put the library name and address and a release date so that the newspaper knows when the library wants the story run. Write a short headline to tell what the story is about and then leave space for an editor to add notes and a headline. Newspaper stories should end with the symbol ###. If the story goes onto a second page, use "-more-" at the bottom of a page. At the end of the story include a name and telephone number so that the newspaper staff can call if they have questions. Any photographs included with news releases should be

good quality prints, printed on black-and-white glossy paper. Attach a caption to the bottom of the picture.

SAMPLE: News Release

From: Paradise County Library
        123 Fourth Street
        Heavenly, South Carolina 29222

For Release July 1, 1989

"Mr. Toad's Adventures" Comes to Paradise County Library

Chopstick Theater of Charleston, South Carolina, will present "Mr. Toad's Adventures," a play for children ages six to twelve at the Paradise County Library on July 8, 1989, at 3:00 P.M. Admission is free, and the performance will last approximately 45 minutes. The library is located at 123 Fourth Street in Heavenly.

"Mr. Toad's Adventures" is an original play developed by the Chopstick Theater. It is based on episodes from Kenneth Grahame's classic children's book *The Wind in the Willows*, about four animal friends. The hero of the play is Toad, a boastful, conceited but good-tempered fellow who is always looking for adventure. However, most of his adventures don't turn out quite as he hoped.

Chopstick Theater is a live theater acting troupe organized in 1983. They have performed at the Spoleto Festival, other community festivals, and in many schools and libraries using a unique style that stimulates the imagination and involves viewers.

For more information contact the Paradise County Library at 999-9900.

###

For further information, contact
        Ima Book, Children's Librarian, 999-9900

Do not try to cover more than one story in a release. It is much better to send individual releases on each program. For a series of programs, do a news release on the series and also for each individual program. This serves to remind people and helps reach those who may not have read the first article. Do not limit news releases to programs, exhibits, and new services. Be alert to other news involving service to children. Perhaps you notice a new trend in what children are reading or a significant increase in requests for help with school research. These can be stories in themselves or useful openings to feature stories.

If possible try to get to know the person on the newspaper staff responsible for library coverage. Libraries which build good working relationships with newspaper staff tend to get better coverage. At the very least identify the person or department where you should address your releases.

Send copies of news releases or announcements to community organizations and agencies and ask them to include the news items in their newsletters. Schools often have parent newsletters and will include information about community services and activities which will enhance student experiences. For the library media center, these newsletters can help to inform parents about its role and activities. Even neighborhood churches may be willing to post information on bulletin boards.

Occasionally the newspaper may be willing to do an interview or to cover an event at the library. In requesting coverage, give the editor enough time to schedule a reporter or photographer and give exact date, time, place, and essential information. If a photographer comes during a program, have someone available to answer questions and identify people.

RADIO AND TELEVISION

Radio and television coverage includes both interviews and public service announcements, more commonly known as PSA's. Some libraries also have their own programming on cable television, or staff members make regular appearances on a program to talk about new books or library events. Radio and television are powerful influences and cannot be ignored. The average American watches several hours of television a day, and when not watching it, may be listening to the radio. Many people listen to the radio and watch television who never read a newspaper or come into the library.

To get short announcements of upcoming activities for children on radio, libraries can send radio stations a shortened version of a news release, including the essential details. Disc jockeys read these between recordings or as part of a community bulletin board report on community events. Often cable television companies have a station running community announcements and will use this same brief information. Keep this type of release less than a page in length.

Another type of PSA focuses not on events but on services and the library's image. There are good quality general PSA's for both radio and television about public libraries produced by the American Library Association, state libraries, and state library associations which are available on tape for reproduction and distribution to local stations. Some of these are aimed at children and parents. They often include well-known people talking about reading and libraries. These can be tagged with a library's name. Often local stations will do this for a minimal charge. Public service announcements focused on a particular library system or event can also be written and either sent to stations in typed form or recorded professionally for stations to play. In planning and distributing PSA's, consider the target audiences of various radio stations and make them appropriate to the audience. Contact stations to find out who is responsible for scheduling them. Ask what they are looking for in a PSA, preferred length and format, and how far in advance the station needs them. This may vary among stations.

Writing good PSA's is not easy. It is important to be sure exactly what you want the announcement to do and to focus only on accomplishing that. Length is strictly limited, and each word must count. At the same time, it must be clever enough to catch someone's attention. It may require a lot of time rewriting and refining. Check with individual stations for their preferred length, but common lengths and approximate number of word are 10 seconds (25 words), 15 (37 words), 20 seconds (50 words), 30 seconds (75 words), and 60 seconds (150 words). Relatively few 60 second spots are used since time is expensive. Thirty seconds is more common. A 30-second spot can be 28 or 29 seconds, but if it is longer than 30 seconds it will not be used. To test length, read it at a pace comparable to that used by stations.

SAMPLE: Public Service Announcement

From: Canton County Library
312 Muncy Ave.
Columbia, Pennsylvania 19920

Jane Jones   To be used beginning
Children's Librarian   Monday June 5, 1989
256-8945   through Friday, June 30,
                             1989

Public Service Announcement

time: 29 seconds

words: 82 words

KIDS WHO GO TO THE LIBRARY IN THE SUMMERTIME HAVE TO BE A LITTLE BIT CRAZY. CRAZY ABOUT HORSES. CRAZY ABOUT ROCK 'N' ROLL MUSIC. CRAZY ABOUT BASEBALL. CRAZY ABOUT MYSTERIES. CRAZY ABOUT FISHING. CRAZY ABOUT MAGIC. CRAZY ABOUT OUTER SPACE. CRAZY ABOUT ANYTHING. IF YOU'RE LOOKING FOR SOMETHING TO DO THIS SUMMER, GET TO THE LIBRARY. YOU MAY GO CRAZY WHEN YOU SEE WHAT'S THERE. CHECK OUT THE MAGICAL MAD HATTER READING PROGRAM AT YOUR CANTON COUNTY LIBRARY. YOU'D BE CRAZY IF YOU DIDN'T.

Use short, descriptive words that are easy to pronounce. Catch the listener's attention before presenting the main message. Try to repeat the main message at least twice. A PSA is used to create interest and to give a broad picture, not to give all the details. After writing, it can be helpful to put it on tape and have several people listen to it. Public service announcements should be typed double- or triple-spaced. Even if the library is supplying a tape, include a typed copy.

Television public service announcements are more complicated because they require visuals to go with the words. Slides are much less expensive than a videotaped spot. Find out if they need to be horizontal or vertical and include a slide for every 10 seconds. Try not to say what the viewer will see. Copy for television needs to be more slowly paced than for radio to allow time to absorb both sight and sound. Plan approximately two words per second. Don't give a station the only copy of a slide. If photographs of people are used, have a release signed by the subjects giving consent for use and stating they do not expect payment or residuals.

Videotaped spots must be filmed and edited with text and visuals perfectly synchronized. Production of these can be quite costly and should be done professionally unless the library has a skilled video department. Remember that on television they are competing with advertisements costing hundreds of thousands of dollars. Making use of taped spots from library organizations for general library promotions is the best way to get affordable high-quality announcements for many libraries.

Make a personal contact when delivering PSA's. Most radio and television stations get more PSA's than they can use, and a personal contact explaining how it will benefit the library, along with interesting text, may help a station decide to use it. If a PSA really catches their attention, it may be run over and over again. It is worth the extra effort to make it as good as possible because if it is not used, all the effort is wasted. Be sure to thank radio and television stations when they do air the spots.

Radio and television interviews are also a good way to reach people. Since they last anywhere from 5 to 30 minutes, there is more time to discuss services or a special program or project. Occasionally, the library may be contacted by a radio or television station for an interview about something the station has heard about. More often, librarians need to contact them when there is something interesting and valuable to share with the community. Become aware of local talk shows with in-studio guests, community service programming, and other programming that feature local events. Many of these programs are actually looking for guests.

In setting up an interview discuss what its focus will be. It may be general, such as what is available for children at the library, or specific, discussing a particular program or new service. However, always be prepared to answer any questions on children's services or the library in general. Do not be made speechless by the interviewer who moves beyond the topic to ask about bad language in books for children. Also, be prepared to fill the time if the topic is adequately covered before the interview is over. Take along a single page of outlined background information that interviewers can quickly scan because in many cases they go into an interview cold and depend on this briefing.

Interviews are essentially conversations. Know the points you want to make and if necessary have a few notes, but do not try to read from a prepared text. Know what you want to say at the beginning and end of the interview to catch listener's attention. Keep answers short and to the point but never just answer yes or no. The interviewer does not want to have to pry information out of you. Use examples to make a point, but don't mention names or exact situations which could be recognizable or embarrassing to someone. Avoid filling silence with "Uh," "You know," and other such phrases. If you are asked an unexpected question, take a few seconds to think rather than jump into an answer. For television interviews take a couple of items that will generate visual interest. After the interview, take time to evaluate how the interview went and decide how it could be better another time.

In considering how the library can use interviews to promote children's services, think about some topics which may be of interest. Perhaps the library has a new parenting collection or is doing a series of programs for parents. Maybe the library is launching summer reading or another special program. During Children's Book Week, a public or school library could schedule interviews with the librarian and a parent to talk about the importance of reading to children.

Sometimes library staff put off making contacts because they hesitate to appear on radio and television. It is not as difficult as it may seem, and it gets easier every time. Most interviewers are friendly and helpful and know how to ask questions to elicit the information you want to share. By not taking advantage of this type of publicity, the children's department is bypassing an excellent way to put its services in the news.

THE IMAGE OF THE CHILDREN'S DEPARTMENT

An important but often overlooked part of the library's public relations program is how people see the library. Appearance and the positive or negative experience people have in the library determine the image of the library and its services.

Look at the physical appearance of the children's area or media center. It should be inviting to a child. A child coming into the public library for the first time should know immediately when they see the children's area. If the children's area is not on the main floor or immediately visible from the library entrance, the signs directing people to the children's area should be inviting and large enough to be seen from an distance. Art or permanent decoration should be appealing to children over a wide age range. It should not appeal only to little children so that older children feel the children's area is not for them anymore. It should also not reflect adult perceptions of what is attractive for children. Either overly sweet, old-fashioned children or cold, modern graphics fit into that category.

The area should be as neat and attractive as possible. Overcrowded shelves with books stuffed in and books falling down because of slipped bookends give a sloppy impression. Housekeeping details can take a lot of time but, if kept up with daily, are not overwhelming. A sloppy room gives an impression that staff doesn't care. If it is necessary to straighten the sports books and picture books every day, then it should be done. Keeping the shelves neat and in order will go a long way toward giving the children's area an inviting appearance. A room that is neat with attractive books on display gives an entirely different impression than one that looks as if no one cares.

The area should have a place where children can get comfortable and read or listen to recordings. The whole area should give the idea that the library is an inviting place. Signs which emphasize what users should not do convey a negative impression. Signs should look neat and professionally done, locations of materials should be clearly labeled, and displays and exhibits should be attractive and timely. A display on winter sports which is still up in April is no longer of interest.

The collection also plays a part in the overall impression. It should be large enough, of good quality, and in good physical condition so that patrons will be able to get what they need when they come to the library. In the same way, the quality of programs for children and the way they are promoted to the public affects perceptions of the library. In schools where children are enthusias-

FIGURE 10. A sculpture or other special feature can add visual interest and give the children's area a distinct personality. (Northwest Regional Branch, Free Library of Philadelphia)

tic about going to the library, teachers will be more supportive of its services.

Patrons' perceptions of the library are often created by the words and attitudes of staff they encounter. A patron's feelings about the children's department can be affected not only by staff in that area but by staff at circulation and reference desks. The entire library staff should respect children and treat their requests as every bit as important as those from an adult. While some of the most creative and exciting activities may happen in the children's areas, these activities often bring more work to other staff. Children rushing in with summer reading records before a program can be a dreaded time for circulation staff. A large turnout for a program means lots of extra books to check in and out. Children are often noisy, stubborn, rude, and not thankful. To other staff it may look as if the children's librarian is having fun doing story hours while other staff are doing work. If staff

develops these types of negative feelings, they may be less likely to talk up programs and services and more likely to be negative to children using the library. Be sure all staff knows what programs are scheduled and why they are important. Enlist their help in letting people know about upcoming events. Thank staff for the help and support they give to work with children.

There should always be someone in or near the children's area or media center who knows children's books well enough to help children find what they want to read. If a child holds up a science fiction story and says, "I want another book like this one," the staff should be able to make suggestions either through their knowledge or use of bibliographies. When the children's librarian or person doing children's programs is out, another staff member should be able to substitute. Arriving at a program only to find out it has been cancelled creates negative impressions on patrons.

Library media specialists can build good relationships within the school by actively working to help teachers. The library media center should also be a place where children can drop in before or after school or during the day. If they can come only on a weekly class visit, they will see the media center just as another class and will not have the opportunity to use it in a leisurely way.

Every part of a library's service plays a role in determining people's attitudes about the library. Without constantly being aware of the total impression services for children give, the library may be giving unintentional negative messages that put children and parents off. General library policies such as inflexible policies for overdue materials, registration, and other requirements may also present barriers to children that give them negative images. Children who feel positively about the library are more likely to be frequent users and to remain library supporters as adults.

BIBLIOGRAPHY

ALA Library Clip Art. Chicago: American Library Association, 1983.

Baeckler, Virginia and Linda Larson. *Go, Pep, and Pop! 250 Tested Ideas for Lively Libraries.* New York: Unabashed Librarian, 1976.

——. *PR for Pennies: Low-Cost Library Public Relations.* Hopewell, NJ: Sources, 1978.

Dodd, Debbie. *Show Your Stuff: Creating Imaginative Library Displays.* Oregon City, OR: EllehCar Press, 1988.

Edsall, Marian S. *Library Promotion Handbook.* Phoenix, AZ: Oryx Press, 1980.

——. *Practical PR for School Library Media Centers.* New York: Neal-Schuman, 1984.

Franklin, Linda Campbell. *Display and Publicity Ideas for Libraries.* Jefferson, NC: McFarland, 1985.

Garvey, Mona. *Library Public Relations: A Practical Handbook.* New York: H. W. Wilson, 1980.

Keefe, Betty et al. "High Touch PR: Practical Approaches to Public Relations." *School Library Media Quarterly* 14 (Spring 1986): 128-130.

Kies, Cosette N. *Marketing and Public Relations for Libraries.* Metuchen, NJ: Scarecrow Press, 1987.

Kohn, Rita and Krysta Tepper. *You Can Do It: A PR Skills Manual for Librarians.* Metuchen, NJ: Scarecrow Press, 1981.

Moran, Irene E., ed. and comp. *Library Public Relations Recipe Book.* Public Relations Sections, LAMA. Chicago: American Library Association, 1978.

Tuggle, Ann Montgomery and Dawn Hansen Heller. *Grand Schemes and Nitty-Gritty Details: Library PR That Works.* Littleton, CO: Libraries Unlimited, 1987.

Relationships with Other Agencies and Organizations

Children's librarians need to be aware of other organizations, community agencies, and schools that are involved with libraries, children, and parents. Good working relationships provide opportunities for cooperation and coordination of activities and for learning about community needs which the library can address.

COMMUNITY AGENCIES

Many agencies, organizations, and individuals working with children and families never consider the library as a resource. Librarians working with children can work to make others aware of library information or services that can help their clients, and as a result stimulate use of the library collection and services. Contacts with community groups may provide opportunities to speak at a meeting, provide a library orientation, or do a special program for a specific group of parents or children. It may also identify individuals who can be resource people for library programs and activities. Working with other agencies and organizations is good public relations which can develop into improved community support for the library.

Local agencies and organizations can be identified through local directories and newspaper articles and by talking with others who work with children. A file of organizations and contact people can be established and added to as staff identifies them.

In some communities, representatives from various groups meet regularly to share information about services for children and to identify needs

not currently being met. If such a group meets in your area, having the library represented will result in better understanding of libraries and their role in the community.

SCHOOL-PUBLIC LIBRARY COOPERATION

Perhaps the most important relationships librarians working with children can develop are with each other. Public librarians and school library media specialists have a great deal of common ground and purpose and should be strong supporters of each other's services. Unfortunately, school and public library cooperation is in many areas nonexistent or minimal. In areas where librarians in both settings have good working relationships and a spirit of cooperation, they have found it results in improved services for children.

A first step is to get to know one another. Public library children's librarians should contact each school librarian in the area and arrange to visit the school library. By seeing the school libraries or media centers in the service area, children's librarians can learn more about similarities and differences and determine what services are unique to each. At each school, they should try to meet the principal, a contact that can prove invaluable for school visits, distribution of flyers, and promotion of public library activities. Likewise, school library media specialists can initiate a relationship by visiting the public library and talking about how it can help students or inviting the children's librarian to a meeting of school district librarians.

In spite of some different priorities, all librarians working with children want to encourage children's reading and use of other materials and help them be comfortable and interested in using libraries. By becoming familiar with each other's services and collections, school and public librarians can promote each other's services. A one-day job exchange, if administrators agree to it, may give both types of librarians better pictures of each other's jobs. At the very least school and public librarians should try to meet a couple of times a year to be aware of what each is doing. At a more involved level, they may form a joint committee for library service to work together on a more regular basis to develop solutions and cooperative efforts.

Once librarians in school and public library settings get to know each other, they realize that they share many of the same problems. Teachers don't always tell library media specialists about major assignments. A class doing a mass assignment can check out all information in both libraries in 24 hours, leaving the other children with no resources. By discussing common problems, school and public librarians can develop a common approach. They could, for example, develop a cooperative brochure for teachers discussing the services each can provide and explaining how teachers can help libraries handle assignment questions and better help students complete requirements. As a team, they can address specific recurring problems in helping students. Too often when the public library contacts a school about problems, it is seen as failure to be supportive of the school's efforts. School librarians on their own may be reluctant to appear not to be supportive of classroom teachers. But when librarians together can show that something is a common problem in terms of how it affects children and suggest some concrete approaches to improving services, response is likely to be more positive. Some public libraries do newsletters for teachers about new resources and special activities for children; they can also discuss what services they can provide for teachers and how teachers can help the library.

Working together on common projects can be explored. School and public librarians can do cooperative reviewing, especially if one or the other receives materials for examination. They may decide to work together on a public relations project to increase awareness of libraries and their role in children's learning, and to make parents aware of the importance of reading, or various other subjects. By including school librarians in summer reading planning, public libraries can build a base for increased school support and perhaps even develop cooperative sponsorship and promotional activities.

Cooperative programming can be developed. For example, a public library could carry a puppet show to a school or invite a school librarian as a guest storyteller. The school library could likewise arrange to let a puppet show done by children be presented at a public library program. They can join together to bring a drama or puppet production or a special speaker to the community. They can work together to provide a library booth and activities at community festivals and fairs and invite each other to workshops and in-service programs. In some areas, school and public librarians plan several cooperative in-service days each year with workshops on topics of common interest.

As relationships between types of libraries become stronger, possibilities for sharing of certain resources may develop. Librarians can talk about interlibrary loan to each other. Some school libraries, for example, loan books to public libraries to meet summer reading demands. A public library may be able to loan materials to a school library media center for a special project. Perhaps one library can agree to purchase certain expensive professional literature and make it available to each other or to loan each other certain audiovisual equipment and resources. The ultimate in school/public library cooperation comes when libraries become willing to share resources for everyone's benefit. It may be hard to justify purchase of an expensive item that will receive little use by individual libraries, but if libraries can agree on one library to purchase it and make it available for all, then all users will benefit.

By developing an attitude that school and public librarians are a team working to provide the best services for all children, librarians can do better jobs and also improve their images and people's understanding of what libraries can do for children and adults alike.

INVOLVEMENT IN PROFESSIONAL ORGANIZATIONS

Librarians working with children should be involved with local, state, and national library associations. Attendance at workshops, meetings, and conventions provides opportunities for continuing education and also for meeting and talking with others. For librarians who work in situations where they are the only person working with children, this interaction can be especially valuable. Participation in committees provides an opportunity to become actively involved and generally offers excellent opportunities for learning as well as contributing to the profession. Most library associations are eager to get new people involved and it is appropriate to ask to be put on a committee. It is not necessary to wait to be asked.

Most librarians cannot attend all the meetings they might like to, but they should be eager to attend when possible. School librarians often have separate associations from the state library association but should try if possible to be involved in other library associations as well. In the same way, public librarians often find it helpful to belong to the school library association. Librarians working with children often limit themselves to the children's services section of library associations. However, they should try to become active in sections that focus on public libraries and administration in order to develop a broader view, to take advantage of the opportunties to learn management and other skills, and to ensure the consideration of services to children as librarians discuss priorities and policies.

Librarians working with children should also consider belonging to other organizations concerned with children. Becoming involved with a group such as the International Reading Association, whose members are largely teachers of reading, or the National Association for the Education of Young Children can provide the opportunity to make many contacts that can benefit the library and to learn about children and learning from a nonlibrary perspective. Most of these organizations have local or state chapters which hold workshops and other meetings. No one person can join and be involved in all relevant organizations. However, choosing to be involved in one or two nonlibrary organizations that focus on children can be very beneficial.

Reaching out beyond the library to the community, the school, and even to other library groups can be time consuming and is often frustrating. It can seem difficult to justify activities which take librarians away from the library. However, the contacts and information gained can bring new clientele into the library and provide librarians with new ideas to improve services.

BIBLIOGRAPHY

ALSC and YASD Liaison Committees, American Library Association. "Directory of National Youth-Serving Organizations." *Top of the News* (Spring 1985): 228-234.

"Community Education: New Directions for School Media and Public Library Programs." *School Library Quarterly* 7 (Fall 1978): 9-32.

Dyer, Esther. *Cooperation in Library Service to Children.* Metuchen, NJ: Scarecrow Press, 1978.

Huntoon, Elizabeth. "Effective School Visits–A Guide." *School Library Journal* 25 (April 1979): 33.

Young, Diana. "School/Public Library Cooperation." *Public Libraries* 18 (Winter 1979): 104-105.

———. "School/Public Library Cooperation—Virginia Style." *Public Libraries* 24 (Summer 1985): 71-73.

Current Issues in Children's Services

Library service to children has had a rich history of reaching out to children and encouraging their use and enjoyment of books and reading. As the twenty-first century approaches, librarians face new challenges in the face of an information and technology explosion in a rapidly changing society. We don't know what library service to children will be like in the future, but it may well be shaped by our responses to the issues and challenges facing librarians working with children today.

With the majority of mothers now working outside the home and the increase in the number of single-parent families, the American family is changing in ways that are affecting the patterns of society and the lives of children. This change also has a major effect on children's access to public libraries and how children can be served in libraries. Many children are spending their preschool days in child care and some type of after-school program once they begin school. There is less time and opportunity for children to visit libraries on their own or with their families.

Unfortunately, many libraries are ignoring this, acknowledging the fact that fewer children are coming to library activities but not making plans to reach children in different ways. If public libraries are going to continue to function successfully for children, they must develop ways to work more effectively with family day care homes, day care and child development programs, and the other institutions where children are. Service to young children may more and more need to be offered through these programs, and many libraries need to take a more active role in indirect service to children by emphasizing training and services to those working with young children.

At the same time that access to libraries is becoming more difficult for many children, there is an increasing realization that illiteracy has its foundations in childhood. There is a reawakened interest in the value of reading. Libraries need to develop ways to work with schools, day care centers, churches, and other community agencies to confront and eradicate this problem.

Many libraries face an increasing problem with so-called latchkey children, whose parents send them to the library after school until they finish work. This presents problems of space and control, and most libraries have not found solutions other than trying to limit it. Some libraries are beginning to use this as an opportunity to involve some of these children in the library. School library media centers are also affected, although less so. They may feel increasing pressure to provide service to children after school hours and to school-based, after-school programs.

At the same time, the number and proportion of children in the population are decreasing in the United States. With fewer children able to get to the library and fewer to come, children's librarians will feel increasing pressure to justify their services as libraries try to serve other growing segments of the population.

Technology presents another major challenge. Information will increasingly be available to people at home and work without the necessity to look it up at the library. At the same time libraries will have sophisticated access to information through databases and to other resources through networking and resource sharing. Librarians working with children must work to ensure that children are included in these new services. Children need to be guaranteed equal access to databases and to resources from other libraries. Libraries along with schools may increasingly function as places where children can get access to technology, important for the many who will not have it at home because of economic reasons. Technology also presents opportunities for school and public libraries to know about each other's resources and greater sharing of them, but librarians need to develop policies that will allow school-owned materials to be used by those outside the school and allow public library materials to be freely used in schools.

The reform movement in American public education presents particular challenges to school library media centers. Libraries may play a central role in increased emphasis on learning or they may be viewed as extras in a day when people want basics. This has been a shadow over the school library community for years. While in many districts they are considered indispensable, in others they are an early target in times of cutbacks. Reform presents an opportunity to show that the library is essential to school success, but if school libraries are left out of funding increases, they may become less rather than more significant in the life of the school and its students.

Library collections also will change significantly in the future as nonprint materials take a larger proportion of the budget. This is an increasingly visual and aural society, and libraries need to acknowledge this change and respond to it. Too often they have buried their heads in the sand, focusing only on the book collection and purchasing a few records and tapes without giving them much time or thought. In the near future, libraries must start putting nonprint materials on an equal footing with print and respond to the way Americans are choosing to get information and recreation. At the same time they need to continue to promote literacy and reading for enjoyment. To do this will require developing a delicate balance.

There is an increasing shortage of trained children's librarians for public libraries. Anyone who has tried to recruit in recent years knows that the days when there were numerous applicants for a single position are gone in many parts of the country. Schools also report a shortage of media specialists. This is due to a combination of factors. Women are increasingly choosing other professions, and those which traditionally attracted women are all facing shortages. Salaries are significantly more attractive in business and industry. Schools attract many of those people who want to work with children either as teachers or media specialists. The education reform movement is resulting in increased salaries in schools, and public libraries have not caught up. A higher salary, more vacation, and no night and weekend work make many librarians choose school rather than public libraries.

At the same time, library schools have increasingly deemphasized service to children. This is partly as a result of lower enrollment in the specialty but also the result of pressure to add faculty in new areas of technology and information science without increasing faculty size. Again and again, as professors leave or retire they are replaced by someone with a different specialty. If people do not receive the specialist training for children's services, few will make it their first choice. For those who do, there will be an increasing need for on-the-job orientation and training programs. A lot has been written about this, but children's librarians and administrators are going to need to deal with this situation more actively. Perhaps we have failed to communicate the skills required for the job in ways that convince people it is a specialty requiring special training. When libraries reduce the number of professionals specializing in children's work or hire someone without training, they reinforce this problem.

These are but a few of the significant issues facing librarians working with children. There are no quick and easy solutions to any of them. Librarians, as a professional body, need to study them and make recommendations. Individual librarians need to begin to develop ways to address them within their own libraries.

Index

Compiled by Estella Bradley

JANE GARDNER CONNOR

Jane Gardner Connor is a freelance writer and children's consultant. She was formerly children's consultant, South Carolina State Library, and has been a youth services librarian. She also gives lectures and workshops to libraries and community groups on the topic of children's books and reading.